China's Cyber Power

Nigel Inkster

China's Cyber Power

Nigel Inkster

ᵀIISS The International Institute for Strategic Studies

The International Institute for Strategic Studies

Arundel House | 13–15 Arundel Street | Temple Place | London | WC2R 3DX | UK

First published June 2016 **Routledge**
4 Park Square, Milton Park, Abingdon, Oxon, OX14 4RN

for **The International Institute for Strategic Studies**
Arundel House, 13–15 Arundel Street, Temple Place, London, WC2R 3DX, UK
www.iiss.org

Simultaneously published in the USA and Canada by **Routledge**
711 Third Ave., New York, NY 10017

Routledge is an imprint of Taylor & Francis, an Informa Business

© 2016 The International Institute for Strategic Studies

DIRECTOR-GENERAL AND CHIEF EXECUTIVE Dr John Chipman
EDITOR Dr Nicholas Redman
EDITORIAL Dr Ayse Abdullah, Jill Lally, Chris Raggett, Nancy Turner
COVER/PRODUCTION John Buck

The International Institute for Strategic Studies is an independent centre for research, information and debate on the problems of conflict, however caused, that have, or potentially have, an important military content. The Council and Staff of the Institute are international and its membership is drawn from almost 100 countries. The Institute is independent and it alone decides what activities to conduct. It owes no allegiance to any government, any group of governments or any political or other organisation. The IISS stresses rigorous research with a forward-looking policy orientation and places particular emphasis on bringing new perspectives to the strategic debate.

The Institute's publications are designed to meet the needs of a wider audience than its own membership and are available on subscription, by mail order and in good bookshops. Further details at www.iiss.org.

British Library Cataloguing in Publication Data
A catalogue record for this book is available from the British Library

Library of Congress Cataloging in Publication Data

ADELPHI series
ISSN 1944-5571

ADELPHI 456
ISBN 978-1-138-21116-2

Contents

ACKNOWLEDGEMENTS

Many people have wittingly or unwittingly helped me with this book. But I would like to single out for special mention Gary Li, Samantha Hoffman, Harriet Ellis, Eneken Tikk-Ringas, Rafal Rohozinski, John Mallery and Alexander Klimburg.

INTRODUCTION

To mark the first meeting of the NETmundial Initiative's Coordination Council, held in São Paolo on 30 June 2015, China Military Online published an editorial observing that:

> Global internet governance can no longer dispense with China. 2014 was the twentieth anniversary of China's accession to the internet ... and, by the end of 2014, China had 649 million users, representing one-fifth of global Netizens. This huge number means that no country in the world can afford to belittle the power of China's internet any longer. Moreover, in line with China's continuing rapid economic development, China's internet industries have developed to the point of being comprehensive, diversified, in-depth and international. Measured by market value, four of the world's top ten internet companies are Chinese ... and the vertiginous speed with which China's internet industries have developed now means that China has become a mainstay of the global internet industry.

The piece went on to state that China's voice would have to be heard on issues of global internet governance, and that the country's policies on the area, as articulated by President Xi Jinping, were attracting growing international support.[1]

The NETmundial event primarily brought together representatives of government, civil society and academia from various parts of the world, aiming to encourage discussions on internet governance and to promote the cyber principles purportedly shared by its attendees. However, the initiative was controversial, having grown out of the Brazilian government's reaction to revelations by rogue National Security Agency contractor Edward Snowden about US electronic espionage around the globe, particularly the alleged monitoring of Brazilian President Dilma Rousseff. The Coordination Council included few representatives from the private sector.[2] But, tellingly, China enthusiastically participated in the event, and the NETmundial Initiative enjoyed the support of both the World Economic Forum and the Internet Corporation for Assigned Names and Numbers. The latter creates and controls what is in effect the address book for the internet, and until March 2016 operated under the aegis of the US Department of Commerce.

The Netmundial forum is just one of a growing number that call into question the status quo of an internet that was built almost exclusively by US corporations, and that has from the outset reflected and espoused Western liberal values. The pioneers of the World Wide Web and the internet, people such as Vint Cerf and Tim Berners-Lee, were motivated by a sense of idealism, believing that the medium would enable citizens around the world to communicate freely, and to exchange knowledge and ideas in ways that benefited all of humanity. This vision has to a significant degree been realised. Global communications have been transformed, and knowledge – a commodity that once was scarce and expensive, and that conferred great power on those able to acquire it – has become cheap, ubiquitous and potentially democratising. However, the internet has also proven to have a dark side, empowering a wide range of malign actors who are no longer constrained by geography, and thereby transforming the global threat landscape.

At the same time, many countries have seen the concept of a global information flow that operated largely outside their control as a challenge to their authority and legitimacy. China and other authoritarian states, especially the Russia of Vladimir Putin, have long been concerned about the security implications of their reliance on information networks almost entirely under the control of the United States and its allies. As early as 1998, Russia introduced a resolution into the UN First Committee on 'Developments in the Field of Information and Telecommunications in the Context of Security'.[3] The resolution was essentially designed to ensure that the issue of cyber security would be addressed in the context of arms control and to emphasise the need for 'information security', the concept that national governments had a right to control content within their sovereign internet spheres. For while the internet purported to be – and in many ways was – borderless, it rapidly became apparent that states could exercise a significant degree of sovereign control through the medium, either by monitoring and filtering content themselves or by demanding that internet service providers and other technology companies did so as a condition of their operating licences.

Global discussions on both internet governance and cyber security have seen the world effectively divide into two camps. One comprises the US and other, predominantly Western, liberal democracies – a group sometimes referred to as the 'like-minded'. They advocate the multi-stakeholder model of internet governance, in which a complex and constantly evolving network of individuals and interest groups come together to address a range of issues. This approach produced the Internet Engineering Task Force, a non-profit group whose membership is open to anyone with the requisite technical qualifications and whose purpose is 'to make the internet work better by providing high quality, relevant technical documents that influence the way people design, use, and manage the Internet.[4] The US and its allies also espouse an open internet that is in principle free of government restrictions on content, while arguing for a focus on network security – to ensure that the internet can function in a reliable, hygienic manner.

The second camp comprises authoritarian states led by Russia and China. While not explicitly dismissing the multi-stakeholder concept, they advocate a much stronger role for national governments in internet governance, particularly in relation to matters of public policy. Their focus on information security is based on the Soviet-era concept of information warfare, in which a state secures its information space to ensure that its narrative goes unchallenged. This group would like to formalise global internet-governance structures within the UN, in a top-down model that gives a decisive role to national governments. The approach tends to play well with the states of the developing world, which have a digital disadvantage and are vulnerable to the powerful, destabilising forces of globalisation for which the internet has become a prime vector. It is in these states that the next wave of internet expansion will take place, mainly through mobile devices. China increasingly provides both the network infrastructure and hardware enabling this expansion.

The country's erstwhile reticence on global internet governance reflected its relatively late adoption of the internet and initial dependence on US information-technology companies to build its capabilities. China's stance was also a function of its long-term strategy of keeping a low profile on foreign policy, which had been subordinated to the pursuit of economic development under Deng Xiaoping's 1979 policy of reform and opening up. Following the crackdown in Tiananmen Square on 4 June 1989, China came close to becoming an international pariah, prompting Deng to develop his '24-character strategy', referred to by the Western media as 'hide and bide'.[5] In the wake of the 1996 Taiwan Strait Crisis, which led to the deployment of two US carrier battle groups near China, this strategy was supplemented by Vice-Premier Qian Qichen's dictum that economic development should take precedence over reunification with Taiwan, and that cooperation with Washington should take precedence over confrontation.

It occurred to few Western policymakers and scholars to reflect on what kind of light China hid under a bushel – or the direction in which that light might ultimately be turned. There was a widespread tendency to underestimate the country's potential or to assume that, as it developed economically and a new middle class emerged, political reform towards a Western democratic model would ineluctably follow. Beijing itself did much to contribute to this perception by promoting the concept of *zhongguo heping jueqi* (China's peaceful rise). First espoused by former Central Party School Vice-President Zheng Bijian at the 2003 Boao Conference, the concept held that China's transition to great-power status could be achieved without the disruption and violence that had accompanied the rise of other states.[6] The idea was reinforced in a documentary series produced by China Central Television entitled *The Rise of Great Powers*.

However, the emerging reality suggests that China may now be embarking on a very different course, raising questions in the minds of many in the Western policy community about the country's potential to disrupt the established global order. Henry Kissinger, architect of Sino-American rapprochement in the 1970s, observed in 2012 that 'enough material exists in China's quasi-official press and research institutes to lend some support to the theory that relations [between Washington and Beijing] are heading for confrontation rather than coopera-tion'.[7] Since the onset of the 2008 global financial crisis, which confirmed for China's leaders that the Washington Consensus had collapsed, Beijing has become more inclined to challenge if not the validity of post-war international institutions then at least the West's perceived domination of these institutions.

President Xi's promotion of the 'Chinese Dream' – which began in 2012, following his accession to the presidency, and to the far more important chairmanship of the Chinese Communist Party – marks a shift away from 'hide and bide' and towards a reassertion of China's historical standing as a major power (even though the term has been couched in language that defies clear interpretation).[8] Beijing's unrequited desire for a 'new kind of great power relationship' with Washington is another indication of this pursuit of greater respect and recognition. China has been increasingly open about its wish to redesign the post-war global architecture to give emerging states greater influence. Meanwhile, a narrative holding that the US is, and always has been, intrinsically hostile towards China and seeks to subvert or overthrow the Communist Party – a message that has always resonated with an inherently paranoid Leninist leadership – has been articulated ever more frequently in China's official and semi-official mass media, particularly with reference to the internet as a potential mechanism for Western subversion.[9]

Some Western analysts have interpreted the new, more assertive China as the product of a decades-long strategy to replace the US as the leading global power by 2049, the hundredth anniversary of the People's Republic. In this view, the ground for China's rise has been prepared through deception and concealment designed to lull the West into a false sense of security.[10] Irrespective of whether China has such a strategy, the country has acquired a global network of interests that it has the means to promote and protect, and thus will be a powerful force for change in the twenty-first century. This is a force that Western policymakers, lacking any knowledge of China's language, culture or history, will struggle to understand or accommodate.

The effects of this shift are already manifest in the cyber domain. What was a relatively benign domain for US information-technology companies when China was racing to catch up with Western nations is beginning to give way to a more restrictive environment. As Beijing introduces new legislation on counter-terrorism, national security and cyber security, these firms are increasingly required to provide the government with source codes and to store Chinese data in China. Efforts are also under way to encourage the indigenisation of information and communications technologies (ICTs) in strategically important areas, such as the banking sector.[11] And while China's social-media scene remains relatively lively, the government has progressively constrained the behaviour of prominent bloggers, and there has been a shift away from Sina Weibo, the Chinese equivalent of Twitter, and towards WeChat, a peer-to-peer system that limits the potential for online issues to go viral.[12] In the debate between openness and security that has been at the heart of China's adoption of ICTs, security now appears to be the dominant preoccupation. Beijing's initially piecemeal, reactive approach to managing the internet has become more proactive and systematic, due to the perception that this is key to continuing China's economic and technical progress, as well as to an awareness of the ways in which the mass aggregation of data can potentially enhance political and social control.[13]

Since the First Gulf War, China's military has seized on the implications of modern ICTs for war fighting, particularly in terms of information warfare. China's official position is that the internet should be used only for peaceful purposes, and that the development and use of cyber weapons should be banned. But the People's Liberation Army has formulated an ambitious strategy for fighting 'local wars under informationised conditions', under which cyber capabilities have become a key component of all military exercises.[14] Much has been written by Chinese and Western scholars on the ways in which China might use cyber capabilities for military purposes, including both deterrence and pre-emption, although there is little in official Chinese doctrine that offers clear guidance on how, and in what circumstances, such capabilities should be deployed.

The area of cyber activity for which China is best known, and somewhat notorious, is espionage. Claims that the Chinese state has sanctioned systematic, broad-spectrum industrial espionage targeting US and other Western corporations are heard almost daily, and as a result are no longer considered newsworthy. Combined with Snowden's revelations regarding China, such claims have significantly contributed to a growing climate of mistrust between Washington and Beijing – to the point that they have become an issue in the campaign for the 2016 US presidential elections.[15] And the methodical nature of such attacks has prompted suggestions that China is engaged in economic warfare against the US, although there is little evidence for this contention.[16]

In contrast, China's potential to shape the future of the internet at a global level has attracted little attention from the West's top policymakers. And this issue may in the long term be more significant than state-sponsored cyber commercial espionage in managing China's rise. As part of the country's strategic shift towards greater assertiveness in global cyber negotiations, Lu Wei, head of the Cyberspace Administration of China and an accomplished propagandist, used the World Economic Forum's summer 2014 meeting in Davos as an opportunity to state clearly Beijing's intent to shape internet governance. He reiterated this position at the World Internet Conference held in Wuzhen the following October.[17] Since then, China has patiently implemented a strategy of making slow, steady gains in multiple fora, creating facts on the ground in support of its agenda and making little secret of its aim to erode the US advantage in the cyber domain.

The components of this strategy can be characterised as: harness the country's user community, the largest in the world, as a throw-weight in demanding that foreign businesses operating in China comply with Chinese restrictions and technical criteria; build and support Chinese technology firms such as Huawei, ZTE and Alibaba; construct and operate information networks in the developing world; create cyber-security partnerships such as that established in early 2015 with Russia; champion within the UN the International Code of Conduct for Information Security, in cooperation with Russia, Tajikistan and Uzbekistan; promote Chinese concepts of global cyber governance and cyber security in multiple international fora; advocate the concepts of cyber sovereignty and information security, in an effort to outlaw the kind of covert cyber intrusions in which the US has a significant advantage; maximise Washington's discomfiture following revelations about covert US cyber capabilities, such as those made by Snowden; and develop a domestic legal regime with an extraterritorial element, so that critics based outside Beijing's jurisdiction can be more easily pursued and silenced.

It remains to be seen whether China will succeed in promoting its agenda, and what the implications of such success could be. But Beijing's achievement of any of its main aims would change both the way in which the internet functions and the way in which states exercise power within that medium. The US and its allies, particularly those within the Five Eyes intelligence alliance (Australia, Canada, New Zealand and the United Kingdom), have until now enjoyed a significant first-mover advantage in their ability to use cyber capabilities in the interests of national security and national advantage. That advantage, though still considerable, is starting to erode quite rapidly. Much of it derives from the ability of the US and the UK to access the major fibre-optic cable networks that carry a significant proportion of global internet traffic, and to benefit from cooperation with major US technology corporations – cooperation that has notably diminished since the Snowden revelations. Meanwhile, the developing world is increasingly wired by China, almost certainly in circumstances that will give the country's intelligence community access to the information transiting those networks. And China will continue to exploit its position as the world's leading manufacturer of ICT equipment to shape global engineering and design standards, and to market its indigenous systems. It is far from unimaginable that China will create a cyber Sinosphere – in effect, a globalised version of something that already exists – that has significant normative influence on global cyber security and governance. The impact of such a development is hard to determine, but, if it were to lead to the establishment of parallel internets or border controls online, the strategic and security implications would likely be profound.

For a Western world that set the framework of the post-war global order and became accustomed to running the show, managing the emergence of China as a major global power was always going to be the greatest strategic challenge of the first half of the twenty-first century. The cyber domain has been a powerful enabler of China's rise, and will be a critical avenue through which the country's emerging power is expressed and exercised. It is impossible to predict the form that this exercise of power will ultimately take, although it is by no means inevitable that China's influence will be malign. Indeed, the emergence of a China that is self-confident, secure and willing to invest in the preservation and policing of the global commons could prove to be a force for good. Thus, it will be increasingly crucial for Western policymakers to have a clear, realistic understanding of China's cyber power, as well as of the effects of this power on both China's and the West's global interests. This book examines China's evolving cyber domain and online culture, alleged large-scale cyber espionage, cyber capabilities in the military and 'hard security' domains, and international cyber policies and strategies, before offering some reflections on how these important new phenomena can be managed and accommodated.

Notes

1 'Quanqiu hulianwang zhili xiankai xin pianzhang, zhongguo cheng zhudao liliang zhi yi', China Military Online, 2 July 2015, http://www.81.cn/jwgz/2015-07/02/content_6565967.htm.

2 Kieren McCarthy, 'Internet Governance Group Pushes on without, er, Internet Organisations', Register, 24 December 2014, http://www.theregister.co.uk/2014/12/24/internet_governance_group_pushes_forward_without_internet_organizations/.

3 Tim Maurer, 'Cyber Norm Emergence at the United Nations – An Analysis of Activities at the UN Regarding Cyber-Security', Belfer Center for Science and International Affairs, September 2011, p. 21, http://belfercenter.

ksg.harvard.edu/files/maurer-cyber-norm-dp-2011-11-final.pdf.

4 Internet Engineering Task Force, 'Mission Statement', https://www.ietf.org/about/mission.html.

5 The most comprehensive version of this strategy is as follows: observe dispassionately; secure our position; deal calmly with events; conceal our capacities and bide our time; cultivate a low profile; never take a leadership role (冷静观察；站稳脚跟；沉着应付；韬光养晦；善于守拙；绝不当头). Deng Xiaoping, Collected Works, vol. 3 (Beijing: People's Publishing House, 1993).

6 Zheng Bijian, 'China's "Peaceful Rise" to Great-Power Status', Foreign Affairs, vol. 84, no. 5, September–October 2005.

7   Henry A. Kissinger, 'The Future of US–Chinese Relations', *Foreign Affairs*, vol. 91, no. 2, March–April 2012, pp. 44–5.

8   'What Does Xi Jinping's China Dream Mean?', BBC, 6 June 2013, http://www.bbc.co.uk/news/world-asia-china-22726375.

9   See Wu Zhenghua, 'Jue buneng rang hulianwang chengwei renxin liushidi', *People's Liberation Daily*, 13 May 2015, http://jz.chinamil.com.cn/gd/2015-05/13/content_6488193.htm.

10 See Michael Pillsbury, *The Hundred-Year Marathon: China's Secret Strategy to Replace America as the Global Superpower* (New York: Henry Holt and Company, 2015).

11 'China Said to Plan Sweeping Shift from Foreign Technology to Own', Bloomberg, 17 December 2014, http://www.bloomberg.com/news/articles/2014-12-17/china-said-to-plan-sweeping-shift-from-foreign-technology-to-own.

12 'Has China Silenced Its Bloggers?', BBC, 12 July 2015, http://www.bbc.co.uk/news/blogs-trending-33464788.

13 Rogier Creemers, 'Internet Plus: Technology at the Centre of Chinese Politics', in European Council on Foreign Relations, *China Analysis*, July 2015, http://www.ecfr.eu/page/-/CA_1507_Governing_the_Web.pdf.

14 Anthony H. Cordesman, *Chinese Strategy and Military Power in 2014: Chinese, Japanese, Korean, Taiwanese and US Perspectives* (Washington DC: Center for Strategic and International Studies, 2014), pp. 121–3.

15 'Hillary Clinton Accuses China of "Stealing US Secrets"', BBC, 5 July 2015, http://www.bbc.co.uk/news/world-us-canada-33399711.

16 James A. Lewis and Simon Hansen, 'China's Cyberpower: International and Domestic Priorities', Australian Strategic Policy Institute, November 2014, pp. 2–4, https://www.aspi.org.au/publications/chinas-cyberpower-international-and-domestic-priorities/SR74_China_cyberpower.pdf.

17 David Bandurski, 'Lu Wei: The Internet Must Have Brakes', China Media Project, 11 September 2014, http://cmp.hku.hk/2014/09/11/36011/.

CHAPTER ONE

Evolution of the Chinese Internet: Freedom and Control

China has spent much of the last 150 years attempting to catch up with scientific and technical advances of the developed world, while maintaining a sense of national self-esteem commensurate with a state that, for most of recorded history, has regarded itself as culturally, economically and in every other way superior to other nations. From a technological perspective, China was for many centuries fully justified in this perception. By the early fifteenth century, the country's advanced technology had brought it to the cusp of an industrial revolution; indeed, for Joseph Needham, a prominent historian of Chinese science, the great mystery was why such a revolution never occurred.

China's sense of self-esteem was sorely tested in its early contact with Western nations, which had acquired a higher level of technology, and was further challenged when Meiji-era Japan, a country traditionally seen as a vassal state, proved an early and successful adopter of this technology. China struggled to make sense of the challenge of modernity, partly because its intellectual culture had focused on the cultivation of moral virtue in the service of governance and social harmony, often spurning mere technical capabilities. The ensuing intellectual turmoil gave rise to a range of responses, including efforts to rediscover the original purity of Confucianism and to reject the West; statesman Zhang Zhidong's concept of *zhongxue wei ti, xixue wei yong* (Chinese learning for substance, Western learning for utility); and the iconoclastic ultra-modernism of early-twentieth-century polemicists such as Hu Shi.

Despite this intellectual uncertainty, which was accompanied by political instability that caused the collapse of the imperial system, China modernised to a greater extent than is often realised – although that process tended to centre on the cities of the eastern seaboard, largely excluding a rural hinterland that resisted change. The drive for modernisation was set back significantly by the 1937–45 Sino-Japanese War and the civil conflict that preceded the founding of the People's Republic in 1949. Mao Zedong's China had a mixed record in scientific and technical development, but his government's investment in basic preventative healthcare and literacy programmes laid an important foundation for future progress. In the 1950s, China derived significant benefits from Soviet technical assistance. And, for a short period following the 1958–60 Great Leap Forward, a return to economic rationality produced respectable annual growth figures of around 4–5%.[1] Nonetheless, intellectuals, particularly scientists, were distrusted for their bourgeois international outlook, and thus subjected to bouts of repression. Mao asserted the importance of both 'redness' – political reliability – and expertise, but his real preoccupation was with class struggle, in which China's intellectuals fared poorly. During the anarchy and institutional degradation of the 1966–76 Cultural Revolution, many scientists were sent to the countryside to undertake manual labour, with the result that scientific research virtually ground to a halt, along with most formal education. The exceptions were nuclear-weapons development and computer science: researchers at the Chinese Academy of Sciences (CAS) produced China's first integrated circuit in 1968.[2]

New economic policy

Following the Cultural Revolution, China's leadership struggled both to stabilise the country and to revitalise an economy that in many respects was functioning almost at subsistence level. In 1978 Deng Xiaoping, the country's leader despite not being formally designated as such, resurrected the concept of the Four Modernisations – agriculture, industry, science/technology and national defence – with the aim of quadrupling China's GDP by the end of the millennium and, ultimately, drawing level with the developed world. At the time, China had no personal computers and little understanding of the advances in computerisation being made in the United States. However, interest in the discipline grew rapidly as the trickle of Chinese students undertaking advanced studies in the West became a flood, and Western companies answered the call to begin investing in China. An important catalyst for the shift was the writing of the US futurologist Alvin Toffler, whose books *Future Shock* and *The Third Wave* were eagerly read in the early 1980s by Chinese intellectuals and leaders, reportedly including Deng and Premier Zhao Ziyang. Toffler was especially prescient in anticipating the transformational effects of information and computerisation on society and the global economy: 'linked to banks, stores, government offices, to neighbours' homes and to the workplace, such computers are destined to reshape not only business, from production to retailing, but the very nature of work and, indeed, even the structure of the family', he wrote.[3]

Jiang Zemin, who would go on to become secretary-general of the Chinese Communist Party (CCP) and president, emphasised the importance of computers in securing a competitive advantage during his 1983–85 tenure as Minister of the Electronics Industry. An engineer by training, Jiang talked of information and communications technology (ICT) as 'the strategic high ground in international competition … the discrepancy between China's level and the world's advanced level is so great that we have to do our utmost to catch up'.[4] Accordingly, Beijing decided in 1983 to prioritise China's electronics industry and to increase its output eightfold under successive Five-Year Plans (double the target growth rate for the wider economy).[5] Shortly thereafter, the CAS invested in a start-up company that evolved into the Legend Group and then Lenovo, now the world's largest manufacturer of personal computers. In 1986 the government established the China Academic Network, linking China's universities. In 1992 China designated the development of the information economy as an important objective; in 1994 it began to take steps towards connecting the country to the internet; and, two years later, it moved to extend internet access to the general population.

Chinese Academy of Sciences

These developments took place amid ideological division within the Chinese leadership on the merits of openness versus social control, a debate that shaped and continues to shape the evolution of China's internet. The violent suppression of the student movement in Tiananmen Square on 4 June 1989, the fall of the Berlin Wall five months later, the subsequent overthrow of communism in Eastern Europe and the collapse of the Soviet Union were seared into the collective consciousness of China's leadership. The events led to a prolonged period of analysis and introspection in Beijing, as the CCP sought to determine what actions were needed to ensure that it would avoid the fate of its fraternal counterparts. A key conclusion was that the Soviet leadership had failed to satisfy the economic aspirations of its people, reinforcing the centrality of China's drive for economic modernisation and with it the imperative to informationise* (although, at the time, the latter was seen as separate to the equally important process of industrialisation). Tiananmen Square also strengthened the Party's determination to remain in control no matter what, and this conviction applied to new information technologies. In contrast to the US government's creation of an environment that enabled the private sector to develop internet technologies and services, Beijing conducted a series of top-down interventions that drove forward the development of the Chinese internet while seeking to strike a balance between the free flow of information and the dictates of national security.

The year 2000 proved galvanic in terms of China's progress towards becoming an advanced informationised society. Following a decade of relative economic liberalisation, the country's Politburo decided that year to make the development of such a society a priority policy goal. A key driver in the Politburo's thinking was its recognition of the changes in China caused by the creation of ever greater quantities of information, and of the need to meet rising social expectations through improvements in transparency and accountability. The conviction that the internet and social media can be used to improve standards of governance, with the aim of nipping social dissatisfaction in the bud, has become an abiding prin-

---

* There is no indigenous Chinese word that equates exactly to 'cyber'. The neologism '赛博' (*saibo*) is used in Chinese translations of Western publications, particularly in relation to cyber warfare, but otherwise has no currency. Initially, the neologism '因特网' (*yinte wang*) was used to translate 'internet', but this has been largely replaced by '互联网' (*hulianwang*), which literally means 'mutual connection network'. 'Cyber security' is usually translated as '网络安全 络安' (*wangluo anquan*), meaning 'network security', or alternatively as '信息安全' (*xinxi anquan*), meaning 'information security'. 'Cyberspace' is generally translated as '网络空间 络空' (*wangluo kongjian*). The processes by which activities become cyber-enabled is denoted by '信息化' (*xinxihua*), meaning 'informatisation', a term that is in widespread use within China and that appears in almost all documents on cyber policy.

ciple of the Chinese leadership. This belief has played a large part in Beijing's approach to information control and censorship. Jiang set the scene for such activities in a speech at the 2000 World Computer Congress widely circulated by state media, arguing that:

> Virtual reality is profoundly changing the way we produce, learn and live … the speed and scope of its transmission has created a borderless information space around the world … The internet also brings problems that make people uneasy: anti-science, false science and information that is unhealthy to the point of being downright harmful.[6]

Jiang was undoubtedly referring to the phenomenon of Falun Gong, a sect based on traditional qigong martial arts and meditation practices, whose adherents had orchestrated the previous year a mass demonstration outside the walls of the Zhongnanhai leadership compound in Beijing. The members of Falun Gong, many of whom were personnel from the People's Liberation Army (PLA) and the police, had used modern ICT to organise the event. Millenarian sects of this kind have frequently played a catalytic role in the overthrow of China's ruling dynasties. Thus, for the CCP, Falun Gong was an existential threat.

During the early 2000s, the Chinese leadership made several major institutional changes. These included the establishment of the State Council Informatization Office, China's Computer Emergency Response Team and the Internet Society of China, a supposedly non-governmental organisation comprising internet service providers, network carriers and various business and academic figures. In 2000 China for the first time sought to develop its information strategy in cooperation with the World

Bank, which subsequently produced a series of frank, hard-hitting reports that identified the shortcomings of Beijing's existing policies. The most recent of these reports, entitled 'China 2030', recommended a series of challenging measures that China would have to implement to become an advanced informationised society.[7] In 2001 the government's 10th Five-Year Plan identified informatisation as a strategic priority. Three years later, the CCP Central Committee published 'Several Opinions on Strengthening the Exploitation and Development of Information Resources', the key finding of which was that these processes should henceforth be driven by market forces. This period of relative liberalisation was reinforced by the 2006 National Informatization Plan, which emphasised, inter alia, the development of laws governing the internet.

These developments were accompanied by a raft of government initiatives in areas such as e-governance and e-commerce, and by a continuing push from then-premier Wen Jiabao to promote open government, using the internet and social media to expose corruption and malpractice among the authorities. This aspect of policy was highlighted in China's first White Paper on the internet, published in 2010. The document spoke of citizens' rights to speak freely, access information and exercise democratic supervision of the government, commenting that 'the leaders of China frequently log onto the internet to get to know the public's wishes and sometimes have direct communications with netizens to discuss state affairs and answer their questions.' The same year, the authorities established the online bulletin board *zhitong zhongnanhai* (Direct Line to the Government), supposedly to enable citizens to communicate directly with the leadership, and China's police forces launched microblogs such as Safe Beijing to facilitate communication with the public.[8] In this period, the government also did a great deal to strengthen legislation relating to intellectual-property protection and the right to privacy. The National People's Congress Standing Committee published in December 2012 its principles of internet privacy, which were translated into regulations issued in July 2013 by the Ministry of Information Industry Technology. The regulations aimed to enforce international standards of data protection with penalties that included fines and even jail sentences.

In its early stages, the development of China's internet was characterised by a period of chaotic creativity similar to that which had occurred in Western countries. Japanese, Taiwanese and US manufacturers were quick to take advantage of China's low labour costs, establishing factories in the special economic zones along China's eastern seaboard, and the country rapidly became the global manufacturing centre for microprocessors and other hardware. By 2003, China had become the world's third-largest manufacturer of ICT products; by 2004, it had become the world's largest manufacturer of laptop computers and mobile phones.[9] Many young Chinese engineers and entrepreneurs who had studied and learnt their trade in the West returned to China, putting their skills and experience to use in establishing a range of indigenous internet services. These included the Sohu and Sina web portals, the NetEase email provider, e-commerce firm Alibaba (which in early 2015 would launch on the New York Stock Exchange) and messaging service Tencent QQ. The contours of the modern Chinese internet emerged with the establishment of service providers such as the search engine Baidu, video services Tudou and Youku, and microblogging site Sina Weibo. These entities provided services similar to those of Western companies, but were able to achieve greater success by better understanding the specifics of the Chinese market. A case in point was Alibaba's Taobao consumer-to-consumer auction site, which by 2006 had driven eBay out of the Chinese market.[10]

The Chinese internet culture that emerged from this period of rapid, chaotic growth was at once similar to and quite distinct from what had evolved in Western countries. One obvious point of difference was language. Although developers created several software systems that enabled users to input text using the strokes that make up Chinese characters – the best-known being Wubi – systems based on pinyin Romanisation created by companies such as Microsoft initially dominated the market. This was something of a paradox, in that the complexities of written Chinese – requiring the recognition of 3,000 characters for basic literacy and more than 10,000 for tertiary education – had long been seen as an impediment to modernisation, to the point where the authorities had seriously considered moving towards the use of a Romanised script. Yet computerisation has arguably given written Chinese a new lease of life, even if it has required users to input text using Roman letters that few were initially comfortable with. Before the adoption of modern ICT, documents in Chinese could only be produced using type-writers that were in effect small printing presses operated by trained specialists. However, computerisation arguably plays to the strengths of a language that is much terser than most of its Indo-European counterparts – conveying more data in less space – and that can be read without an understanding of how words should be pronounced, making for more efficient storage and transmission.

Chinese search engines have always been colourful and crowded, requiring users to do little more than click on the items that interest them most. For Chinese netizens, the internet has long been a source of entertainment – in the form of music, films, dating and gaming. By 2009, online gaming generated revenues of 25.8 billion RMB (US$4.7bn),[11] and was so pervasive that the government was driven to outlaw the use of virtual currencies to purchase physical goods.[12] The PLA made a virtue of necessity by permitting its soldiers to engage in online gaming, on the basis that this would enhance their capacity for strategic thinking.[13] But perhaps the most significant development in China's internet was the emergence of microblogging sites such as Sina Weibo, combined with massive growth in the use of smartphones. By 2014, 89% of China's 668 million internet users accessed the internet via mobile devices and, by the following year, Chinese firms sold such devices with greater variety, functionality and flexibility – and more cheaply – than most Western service providers.[14] Despite being illegal, pornography proliferated on the Chinese internet to the point that even the most innocuous websites contained raunchy adverts for services such as male enhancements – one click on which would take the user to a video illustrating in explicit terms their supposed benefits. Since 2010, the authorities have progressively closed down pornographic websites in successive clean-up campaigns. And, although China's low-trust society meant that few citizens initially owned credit cards, e-commerce accounted in 2014 for 10% of retail sales of consumer goods, or 12.3 trillion RMB (US$2trn), a figure that was expected to double by 2018 (the bulk of this trade was business-to-business).[15]

Technology and indigenous innovation

By 2000, China's ICT sector was growing at twice the rate of the rest of the economy, primarily due to foreign direct investment and start-up activity by young Chinese returnees. Due to the growth of private companies, the proportion of the ICT sector owned by the state fell by roughly half.[16] China was well on the way to becoming the world's largest ICT manufacturer. But there was already a powerful imperative for the country to move up the value chain as a means of avoiding the middle-income trap, and China's leaders were aware that it would take more than manufacturing capabilities to create an advanced informationised society. The approach they adopted initially emphasised building the ICT infrastructure that would form the basis of further developments. Yet, as highlighted by the first of the series of World Bank reports commissioned by the State Council, they also recognised that China would need to transform its higher-education system and its approach to research and development.

In 2000 China's education system was nowhere near good enough to produce the skilled workforce needed to realise the country's ambitions. Spending on education was just 2.5% of GDP; only 11% of the population participated in tertiary education; and, among China's small number of PhD candidates, few focused on information technology. The decade that followed was transformative: the number of PhD students quadrupled, the number of institutes providing tertiary education doubled and there was a massive increase in the number of Chinese students enrolled in university courses overseas.[17] The CCP's 2010 National Plan for Medium and Long-term Education Reform and Development set the strategic objective of 'rejuvenating the country through science and education, making the nation strong by relying on talents and professionals, running education to the satisfaction of the people and building a rich resource of human talent'.[18] Nonetheless, the story of the growing numbers of Chinese graduates obscured important issues, particularly the poor quality of China's education system and the pervasive nature of bureaucratism within China's universities. The latter fact was acknowledged by the CCP Central Committee in 2013, when it spoke of the need to 'smash administrative dominance' within China's research and development culture[19] – apparently ignoring the connection between this culture and the Party's own record of imposing rigid intellectual and political orthodoxy.

A major driver for indigenous innovation in China has been a constant awareness of both the security vulnerabilities of near-total dependence on ICT products designed abroad – primarily in the US – and the internet's potential as a vector for subversion. Since Deng's approval in 1986 of the technology-focused 863 Plan, which was quickly extended to cover ICTs, *zizhu chuangxin* (indigenous innovation) has been a mantra for Chinese leaders working to modernise strategically important industries. As early as 2006, the State Council's Medium and Long-term Guidelines Programmes for Science and Development identified reliance on foreign technology as a threat to China's economic and national security.[20] Starting in 2009, Beijing made successive efforts to build indigenous innovation into state programmes for procuring ICTs, and to develop indigenous technical standards to exercise more effective sovereign control over such technology. Numerous Chinese ICT corporations began to emerge: Inspur and Sugon in high-end servers; Lenovo in personal computers; Loongson in central processing units for personal computers; Rockchip and HiSilicon in central processing units for mobile devices; Huawei and ZTE in high-end routers, switches and cloud computing; Kingsoft in office software; Qihoo 360 in anti-virus software; NeoKylin in operating systems; Yonyou and Kingdee in management software; and Baidu in internet search and browsers. Meanwhile, China has made an effort to promote the development of software systems based on Unix, and has been quick to exploit the potential of the IPv6 internet protocol.[†] But, to date, Chinese companies have struggled to replace the

---

† The Internet Engineering Task Force designed Internet Protocol Version 6 in the 1990s as a replacement for Internet Protocol Version 4, the first publicly available internet protocol. An internet protocol is a unique identifier – in effect, an address – for online devices and, together with the transmission control protocol, enables communication between these devices.

American products on which China relies. This was demonstrated in 2014, when Microsoft's announcement that it would withdraw security support for Windows XP generated such consternation in China that the company was forced to reconsider, and to treat the country as a special case.[21] An August 2014 article in the China Financial and Economic National News Network set out a litany of complaints from China's ICT firms: pressure from US competitors and discrimination against Chinese companies in international markets; a taxation structure that continued to privilege foreign companies; and the unwillingness of state entities to purchase indigenous products even where they were competitive, due to heavy investment in foreign systems.[22]

Information control

A focus on the control of information has always been a key driver of China's policies on the internet, which were initially reactive, fragmented and often at odds with one another. In 1994, the year the internet became publicly available, the Chinese authorities promulgated the Regulations on Security and Computer Information Systems, giving the Ministry of Public Security, China's police service, responsibility for policing Chinese citizens online. The State Council approved in 1997 the Computer Information Network and Internet Security, Protection and Management Regulations, banning online incitement to resist or break the constitution, laws or administrative regulations; incitement to overthrow the government or the socialist system; incitement of division in the country or efforts to obstruct national reunification; incitement of hatred or discrimination against national minorities; dissemination of falsehoods, distortions of the truth, rumours or messages that disrupt social order; promotion of feudal superstitions, sexually suggestive material, gambling, violence or murder;

promotion of terrorism and incitement of other criminal activities, including insulting and slandering people; attacks on the reputation of state organisations; and any other activities which ran counter to the constitution, laws or administrative regulations.[23] This characteristically wide-ranging list gave China's security services almost limitless scope to take action against entities and individuals they wished to silence.

The authorities were particularly eager to filter out externally generated content via the Golden Shield project, which was introduced in two phases – 1998–2006 and 2006–08 – under the direction of Fang Binxing, president of Beijing University of Posts and Telecommunications and a member of the Chinese Academy of Engineering. Often referred to in the Western media as 'the Great Firewall of China', the Golden Shield uses IP blocking, DNS filtering, URL filtering, packet filtering and SSL 'man-in-the-middle' attacks to prevent 'unhealthy' content from entering China through one of the country's six international internet exchange points. Some websites, such as that of the BBC, were permanently blocked, while others were selectively filtered. Residents of China who wished to bypass Golden Shield were initially able to do so by joining virtual private networks but, over time, the authorities progressively restricted use of these systems, as well as online libraries, text-messaging applications and cloud-computing services. The Internet Society of China was able to nudge indigenous service providers towards implementing policies in the manner the government intended, but their Western counterparts struggled to reconcile a desire to abide by China's laws and practices with core values, especially the principle that the flow of information must be free. This tension proved unbearable for Google, which opted in 2010 to leave its offices in mainland China and relocate to Hong Kong.[24] Meanwhile, the blocking of major Western social-media platforms such as Facebook and Twitter channelled all social-media commentary through domestic microblogging sites such as Sina Weibo and WeChat.

In addition to blocking information generated abroad, the government faced the more challenging task of managing content generated within China, particularly once the use of microblogging services had begun to create a tsunami of online commentary covering personal, local, national and foreign-policy issues. In a country whose leadership has always been deeply suspicious of civil-society groups, China's netizen community has become a form of civil-society group that highlights a range of grievances, including high-handed behaviour by corrupt and hitherto unaccountable officials. A case in point is that of Li Qiming, son of the deputy head of the Baoding Public Security Bureau, Li Gang. In October 2010, Li Qiming, driving while drunk through the campus of Hebei University, struck two female students, killing one and seriously injuring the other. Having been prevented from escaping the scene by students and campus security guards, Li Qiming is alleged to have said 'sue me, if you dare: my father is Li Gang'. The episode went viral on Chinese social media, leading to the arrest of Li Qiming, and prompting his father to appear on local TV to ask the families of the victims for forgiveness. 'My father is Li Gang' entered popular usage as a catchphrase for anyone seeking impunity. In 2012 Yang Dacai, the senior official responsible for work safety in Shaanxi Province, was photographed smiling at the scene of a serious road accident, wearing a wristwatch whose value was many times his annual salary. A *renrou sousuo* (human flesh search) conducted by netizens revealed photographs of Yang wearing a variety of equally expensive timepieces. Yang, who subsequently achieved notoriety with the epithet *biaoge* (Brother Watch), was investigated and sentenced to 14 years in prison for corruption.[25] Such online activism has also highlighted major public-safety episodes that

China's officials initially sought to downplay, including the crash of a high-speed train in Wenzhou in 2011 and an explosion at a chemical-storage warehouse in Tianjin in 2015. In both cases, the authorities' attempts to limit information and manage the public reaction were frustrated by pervasive online reportage that led to demonstrations.

China's netizen community has been equally vociferous on foreign-policy issues. This can be largely attributed to the Patriotic Education Programme introduced into Chinese schools following Tiananmen Square as a means to inculcate in citizens a sense of nationalism and historical grievance. Accordingly, China's online activists condemned those they saw as having offended the country, in episodes such as the 2001 collision between US EP-3 surveillance aircraft and a PLA Air Force fighter off the coast of Hainan; UN Secretary-General Kofi Annan's March 2005 statement that Japan should be considered for a permanent seat on the UN Security Council; and protests in Western countries in support of the Free Tibet movement in the run-up to the 2008 Beijing Olympics. These confrontations included efforts by patriotic Chinese hacker groups such as the Honker Union to damage foreign websites, a phenomenon that led in 2001 to a week-long hacker war between China and the US – which ended only after Beijing instructed Chinese hacker groups to desist. During the 2005 anti-Japanese demonstrations in China, there were numerous public rallies and attacks on Japanese commercial and diplomatic premises. Three years later, Chinese consumers conducted a national boycott of the Carrefour supermarket chain in protest at the French government's dealings with the Dalai Lama.

The Chinese government has sought to strike a delicate balance between allowing such outpourings of nationalist sentiment to run while ensuring they do not spill over into protests against the regime. Beijing seemed close to losing that balance in 2005, when the anti-Japanese demonstrations morphed into protests about the leadership's perceived weakness in relation to Tokyo. A typical blog post from the time read 'how can China stand firm when its leaders are all impotent? If China gives approval [for Japan's accession the Security Council], this time the state leaders have no right to sit in their current positions – let them go home and embrace their children.'[26]

In March 2000, US President Bill Clinton famously likened Chinese efforts to censor the internet to trying to 'nail Jell-O to the wall'.[27] Since the internet came to China, the country's security services have been engaged in a cat-and-mouse game with netizens seeking to express themselves freely and to access the information they need. One product of this game has been a counterculture of cyber dissidence with its own vocabulary, exploiting the infinite capacity of the Chinese language to generate homonyms and puns as a way of getting round the use of banned terms. Included in this vocabulary are the terms '河蟹' (*hexie*), meaning 'river crab', referring to the censors who seek to harmonise '和谐' (*hexie*) online content; and the pervasive '草泥马' (*caonima*) – literally 'grass-mud horse', a mythical creature resembling an alpaca – as a homonym for '肏你妈', meaning 'fuck your mother', a popular and understandable reaction to the activities of the censors. But censorship of online content has become more advanced and intrusive, to the point that a Chinese blogosphere that was once intensely vibrant and wide-ranging has become, if not sanitised, then certainly much tamer than in the past.

China's mechanisms for censoring domestic online content are complex, multilayered and labour-intensive – and increasingly enabled by technology. Laws and regulations require service providers to police the content on their networks, and the Internet Society of China has played an important role in marshalling its members in support of this objective. Although administrative and legal requirements such as compulsory real-name registration were initially imposed in a somewhat haphazard fashion (like many Chinese laws and regulations), they have been progressively applied with greater consistency. Online censorship is overseen by the Ministry of Public Security and implemented through its hierarchy of provincial, county and municipal entities. There are no reliable public figures for the number of individuals engaged in online censorship, but one report by Chinese state media averred that there were two million, including both private-sector and state employees.[28]

While basic, labour-intensive keyword searches remain a significant component of this censorship effort, they are increasingly combined with advanced data-mining tools that have greatly increased the efficiency and speed of the process. A 2013 study of Sina Weibo showed that 30% of messages deemed to have been unacceptable were deleted within 5–30 minutes of posting, and 90% were deleted within 24 hours.[29] Examples of this kind of material were provided by the online commentary on the 2014 Occupy Central movement in Hong Kong, which protested against government-imposed restrictions on the election of the territory's chief executive with terms such as 'Hong Kong', 'barricades', 'Occupy Central' and even 'umbrella' (used by Hong Kong protesters to protect themselves from tear gas, the umbrella became the icon of the Occupy Central movement). All of these terms were deleted by Chinese censors, as were photographs of President Xi Jinping carrying an umbrella. And, during the 3 September military parade in Beijing marking the 70th anniversary of the end of the Second World War, the authorities censored pictures of Winnie the Pooh – to whom Xi had been compared, on the basis of a photo showing him walking alongside US President Barack Obama during their 2013 summit in Sunnylands. The activities of official censors are supplemented by those of a volunteer 'Civilization Army' of university students, and the work of civilian bloggers known as the *wumaodang* (fifty-cent party), a name derived from the sum they supposedly receive for publishing a pro-government post. These activists deploy a variety of techniques, ranging from a reasoned rebuttal of posts deemed unacceptable to attacks on the integrity and patriotism of the authors of such material.

The Chinese approach to censorship is much more nuanced than is often portrayed in the Western media and, although there has been a progressive tightening of control, Chinese citizens are still able to publicly vent their spleen against official-dom – albeit while remaining uncertain whether a government red line has been crossed, inviting official retribution. China's authorities have been concerned not with criticism of the government per se, but rather evidence of intention to organ-ise or take action outside of CCP and state structures. In 2013 a group of foreign researchers set up their own social-media network in China, thereby gaining access to censorship soft-ware, documentation and customer service help desks. They discovered that 'criticisms of the state, its leaders and their policies are routinely published, whereas posts with collective action potential are much more likely to be censored – regard-less of whether they are for or against the state.'[30] An example of the kind of post that is permitted is:

> The Chinese Communist Party made a promise of democratic, constitutional government at the begin-ning of the war of resistance against Japan. But after sixty years that promise has yet to be honoured. China today lacks integrity, and accountability should be traced to Mao ... intra-party democracy ... is just an excuse to perpetuate one-party rule.[31]

American researcher Rebecca MacKinnon has characterised China's management of online content as 'networked authoritarianism'. As she stated in her testimony before the 2010 US–China Economic and Security Review Commission:

> This new form of Internet-age authoritarianism embraces the reality that people cannot be prevented from accessing and creating a broad range of Internet content. Networked authoritarianism accepts a lot more give-and-take between governments and citizens than a pre-Internet authoritarian regime. The regime uses the Internet not only to extend its control but also to enhance its legitimacy. While one party remains in control, a wide range of conversations about the country's problems rage on websites and social networking services ... As a result, people with Internet or mobile access have a much greater sense of freedom – and may even feel like they can influence government behaviour – in ways that weren't possible under classic authoritarianism. It also makes people a lot less likely to join a protest movement calling for radical political change. Meanwhile, the government exercises targeted censorship, focusing on activities that pose the greatest threat to the regime's power. It also devotes considerable resources to seeding and manipulating the nation's online discourse about domestic and international events.[32]

This assessment remains broadly accurate, but since 2010 there has been growing evidence that China's authorities have increasingly sought to constrain the scope of online discourse, and to use their growing domination of the relevant technologies as means for adopting a more proactive, aggressive approach to shaping that discourse. This has coincided with efforts by the CCP to create a climate of greater intellectual orthodoxy, an effort that became apparent during the second half of Hu Jintao's 2002–12 tenure as CCP secretary-general, and that has accelerated markedly since Xi replaced him.

Rule by law

Xi's appointment was a matter of significant contention among the leadership. Hu had wanted Li Keqiang, who would eventually be appointed prime minister, to succeed him. But there was within the upper echelons of the Party a sense of disappointment with the second half of Hu's tenure: a conviction that progress towards economic modernisation had stalled and that vested interests had become a barrier to progress, with some state-owned enterprises effectively becoming states within the state. The Party was also growing concerned about the public's reactions to pervasive corruption and began to see them as an existential threat to its hold on power. A further complicating factor was the rise of Bo Xilai, CCP Secretary of Chongqing and, like Xi, a 'princeling' (the nickname given to children of the founding members of the People's Republic). As CCP secretary of one of China's largest cities, Bo became a national icon through his New Left programme of welfare reform, social-housing construction, operations against organised crime and Maoist-era mass-mobilisation tactics, which included a 'red songs' campaign. Yet he was brought down by a scandal that began when Wang Lijun, Chongqing's police chief, unsuccessfully sought asylum in the US consulate in the city. Wang Lijun revealed the involvement of Bo's wife in the murder of British businessman Neil Heywood, and admitted to having intercepted the communications of China's top leaders at Bo's instigation. Bo was subsequently removed from office and eventually sentenced to life in prison for corruption and abuse of power, while his wife received a suspended death sentence for her role in the Heywood murder.[33] However, it is likely that, in the eyes of his peers, Bo's real crime was ostentatious self-promotion in a political culture that emphasised self-effacement as the traditional route to the top.

From the outset, Xi adopted a leadership style very different from those of his two immediate predecessors. An important feature of his tenure has been a major campaign against corruption, which has led to the conviction of senior leaders such as former security chief Zhou Yongkang and General Xu Caihou, head of PLA logistics. The sustainment of the anti-corruption drive for more than three years confused and enervated many Chinese officials, who had grown accustomed to such campaigns running out of steam relatively quickly. As a consequence, some of the more talented among them decamped to the private sector. Xi discussed the need to control public morality and popular opinion in a speech in early 2013, stressing the importance of, inter alia, 'consolidating and boosting mainstream public opinion, propagating the leitmotifs [of socialism with Chinese characteristics] and spreading positive energy'.[34] Xi established a pattern of taking direct responsibility for many aspects of government through the establishment of leading small groups (LSGs). One of the most significant of these was the *zhongyang wangluo anquan he xinxihua lingdao xiaozu* (Leading Small Group for Cybersecurity and Informatization), established on 27 February 2014 (see Table 1.1). Xi highlighted the extent of Beijing's ambition in a speech inaugurating the new LSG, speaking of China's need to transform from a *wangluo daguo* (large internet country) into a *wangluo qiangguo* (strong internet country).[35]

The organisation subsumed the responsibilities of two erstwhile LSGs chaired by the prime minister, and received administrative support from the State Internet Information

Table 1.1: **Founding members of the Leading Small Group for Cybersecurity and Informatization**

Xi Jinping (Chair)	CCP General Secretary, Chinese President
Li Keqiang (Vice-Chair)	Chinese Premier
Liu Yunshan (Vice-Chair)	Chief Secretary, CCP Central Secretariat; Chairman, Central Leading Group for Ideology and Propaganda
Lu Wei	(Head, Leading Group Office) Director, Cyberspace Administration of China
Ma Kai	Vice-Premier
Wang Huning	Director, CCP Policy Research Office
Liu Qibao	Director, Central Propaganda Department
Fan Changlong	Vice-Chairman, Central Military Commission
Meng Jianzhu	Director, Central Political–Legal Committee
Li Zhanshu	Director, CCP General Office
Yang Jing	Secretary-General, State Council
Zhou Xiaochuan	Governor, People's Bank of China
Wang Yi	Minister of Foreign Affairs
Fang Fenghui	PLA Chief of Staff
Lou Jiwei	Minister of Finance
Cai Wu	Minister of Culture
Yuan Guiren	Minister of Education
Miao Wei	Minister of Industry and Information Technology
Guo Shengkun	Minister of Public Security
Xu Shaoshi	Chairman, National Development and Reform Commission
Wang Zhigang	CCP Secretary, Ministry of Science and Technology
Cai Fuchao	Director, State Administration of Press, Publication, Radio, Film and Television[36]

Office. The latter was set up in 2011 and renamed the Cyberspace Administration of China in 2014, under the leadership of Lu Wei, a former Xinhua journalist who also served as deputy head of the CCP's Central Propaganda Department. The establishment of the LSG demonstrated Chinese leaders' desire to pull together the different strands of China's informatisation programme, and their recognition of the centrality of the internet to the country's economic, social and political development. The move also appeared to reflect their aim to control online debates on the issue of constitutionalism, or the subordination of the CCP to the rule of law.

On the face of it, the debate accorded with the position Xi himself had advocated since coming to power. In a speech to celebrate the 30th anniversary of China's 1982 Constitution, the president observed that 'no organization or individual has the special right to overstep the Constitution and law, and any violation of the Constitution and law must be investigated.'[37] And one of Xi's *sige quanmian* (Four Comprehensives) – announced amid much fanfare in early 2015 as his contribution to Marxist–Leninist ideology, which every Chinese leader is expected to make – is *yi fa zhi guo* (using law to govern the country). However, the limits of the CCP's tolerance of constitutionalism and the rule of law, in this context perhaps better translated as 'rule by law', were made clear by the release in mid-2013 of Document Number 9. This document listed what became known as the *qige bujiang* (seven taboo subjects): universal values, freedom of speech, civil society, civil rights, the historical errors of the CCP, crony capitalism and judicial independence.[38] Document Number 9 gave rise to a government media campaign that sought to highlight the need for ideological correctness, particularly with reference to the impact of the internet.[39] The effort focused on the 'Big Vs', celebrity bloggers and public intellectuals who each had tens of millions of Sina Weibo followers. In 2014 Chinese courts handed down prison sentences to prominent Big Vs such as Charles Xue Biqun, Qin Zhihui and Yang Xiuyu, after they were convicted of spreading rumours for personal gain – a crime defined as posting false information that is re-tweeted more than 500 times or viewed by more than 5,000 people. One consequence of this pressure was a large-scale move away from the use of Sina Weibo and towards WeChat, a site operated by Tencent on which blog posts could be seen by a maximum of 100 followers. The message from the government was clear: if a choice was to be made between freedom of expression and political control, the latter would always predominate.

New cyber legislation

As well as working to strengthen their control of online content and behaviour for political reasons, the authorities also recognised the need to clean up China's cyberspace. Their prioritisation of content control, or information security, came at the expense of network security, with the result that China's online environment remained anarchic and lawless. Online fraud, data theft, blackmail and libel were common. Reliable statistics are hard to come by but, according to the Ministry of Public Security, there was a 30% increase in online fraud every year from 2011 to 2014, leading to losses of more than 10bn RMB (US$1.57bn) in that period.[40] In December 2012, the National People's Congress Standing Committee formally recognised the need for a more hygienic, better-regulated environment, publishing the Decision Concerning Network Information Protection to promulgate data-protection standards.[41] Since then, a stream of articles in state media outlets have argued for strengthening the rule of law online, putting much emphasis on the responsibilities and moral behaviour of individual users. A *People's Daily* editorial published in October 2014 gives a sense of the discourse:

> As for ordinary netizens, their most fundamental responsibility is to respect the law, act lawfully online, not transgress legal red lines and avoid breaching the limits of good moral behaviour. A higher demand on ordinary netizens is to put out a good Chinese voice, promote positive energy and strive to be 'a good Chinese netizen'. The internet is not outside the law and citizens when they are online must constantly nurture a law-based outlook. Everyone has the right to speak freely and express their opinions but at the same time they must observe discipline: one person's freedom cannot be built on another's lack of freedom. Beyond this, netizens must have a sense of self-discipline and responsibility, promote the common good,

adopt their country's stance, enthusiastically enter into the dance with the current era in order to better promote human values.[42]

In his capacity as China's cyber czar, Lu announced the 'four haves' of the good Chinese netizen during the June 2015 Awareness Week for National Cybersecurity. These are: a high sense of security; a commitment to a civilised online culture that promotes core socialist values; a readiness to obey the law; and the skills to protect oneself.[43]

The Chinese state furthered its plans to develop the internet as a force multiplier and systems integrator for economic development in March 2015, with Premier Li Keqiang's announcement of the concept of Internet Plus. This was followed in July that year by an action plan under which Internet Plus would

> integrate mobile Internet, cloud computing, big data and the Internet of Things with modern manufacturing, to encourage the healthy development of e-commerce, industrial networks, and Internet banking, and to help Internet companies increase their international presence … The action plan maps development targets and supportive measures for key sectors, which the government hopes can establish new industrial nodes, including mass entrepreneurship and innovation, manufacturing, agriculture, energy, finance, public services, logistics, e-commerce, traffic, biology and artificial intelligence.[44]

This plan has given rise to much work on the details of its implementation by a range of ministries and regulatory bodies, as well as proposals for a significant upgrade of the country's internet infrastructure. At the same time, the authorities have put forward a wealth of draft legislation on internet governance. International observers have often interpreted these developments as part of a coordinated effort to limit access to the Chinese market for foreign service providers, and to further restrict online freedom of expression within China. The first piece of draft legislation, issued by the China Banking Regulatory Commission, requires banks operating in the country to increase the proportion of their information-technology products that are 'secure and controllable' (a concept that remains ill-defined) by 15% per year, with the aim of ensuring that at least 75% of these products meet the requirement by 2019.[45] The commission's proposals elicited protests from Washington, US companies and the American Chamber of Commerce in Beijing, which complained that such requirements were discriminatory and would jeopardise intel-lectual-property rights. The regulations were subsequently withdrawn for further consideration, but China's determina-tion to reduce its dependence on Western technology is such that they will almost certainly be revived.

The government passed in December 2015 the first of these new bills related to cyber issues: a counter-terrorism law that required, inter alia, all telecommunications and internet service providers to supply encryption information to Chinese law-enforcement agencies. The original draft of the bill speci-fied that these firms must install back doors in their products, but this provision was later removed. The new legislation built on a national-security law passed the previous July, which in many ways resembled measures implemented by other states to take account of new security risks and threats. However, Article 59 of the law was heavily criticised abroad for its alleged discrimination against foreign companies, as it mandated national-security reviews for all foreign invest-ments that 'impinge on or may impinge on national security', as well as for foreign investments involving key materials or technologies, including information-technology products and services.[46] The legislation was also criticised for its vague definition of national security – although the laws of most states could be found guilty on that charge. This was followed in July by a draft cyber-security law that emphasised the importance of establishing and maintaining 'internet sovereignty', and that set out broad prohibitions on any person or organisation using the networks to engage in 'harming national security, propagating terrorism and extremism, inciting ethnic hatred and discrimination, disseminating obscene and sexual information, slandering or defaming others, and upsetting the social order'.[47] The draft stated that internet service providers would be required to take measures to protect users' personal data, but also to block and report illegal activity, and to ensure real-name registration. It also required the Cyberspace Administration of China to approve all activities relating to the transfer and storage of personal data, and proposed that all such data be stored within the country.

It remains unclear how these new laws will actually operate. Chinese laws tend to be written in sweeping terms, and the manner in which they are enforced is determined by the *guize* (implementing rules) drawn up by relevant ministries. Much of the new legislation forms part of a long-overdue rationalisation and modernisation of China's legal patchwork, which left the country with no effective definition of cyber criminality. And many of the provisions do no more than codify established practices – or, in the case of real-name registration, reinforce efforts to implement existing law. Moreover, as Chinese officials aptly point out, many of the procedures they are seeking to implement mirror arrangements such as the US government's Common Criteria for Information Technology Security Evaluation in projects involving national security. As a consequence of such measures, Huawei and ZTE are banned from bidding for contracts to provide core networks in the US and Australia – and, in the United Kingdom, Huawei is subject to uniquely rigorous security inspections of all its hardware and software, including source code. The Chinese authorities claim that the new laws are not primarily designed to exclude foreign ICT products from China or to isolate the country, and that they need to take measures to secure their networks, particularly following the revelations about US electronic espionage made by rogue National Security Agency contractor Edward Snowden.[48] Lu summed up the position as:

> Foreign Internet companies entering China must at the base level accord with Chinese laws and regulations. First, you can't damage the national interests of the country. Second … you cannot harm the interests of the Chinese consumer. If China's laws and regulations are respected, we welcome all the world's Internet companies to enter the Chinese market.[49]

While China seeks greater confidence in the security of its ICT systems, Chinese officials know that they will remain dependent on foreign systems for some time to come. While Chinese companies have been working to catch up with advanced foreign technologies, these technologies have continued to be superseded, a situation reminiscent of Zeno's paradox of Achilles and the tortoise. The result is a struggle to balance the desire for effective cyber sovereignty – control over systems and content – with the imperative of maintaining access to the advanced technologies key to an ambitious social and economic agenda. China has sought to address this challenge in several ways. The first is the ingenious use of ICT to covertly acquire many of the technologies it sees as critical to economic development and national security, including advanced military capabilities. The second is the use of the country's growing economic and political influence, combined with an indigenous ICT sector whose national champions are competitive in global markets, to shape an international cyber-governance and -security agenda that accommodates Beijing's interests and concerns.

Notes

1   Anton Cheremukhin et al., 'Six Questions about China's Rise from 1953', Vox, 2 September 2015.

2   Greg Austin, Cyber Policy in China (Cambridge: Polity, 2014), p. 23.

3   Alvin Toffler, The Third Wave (London: Pan Books, 1981), p. 152.

4   Jiang Zemin, On the Development of China's Information Technology Industry (Beijing: Central Party Literature Press, 2010), p. xvi.

5   Austin, Cyber Policy in China, p. 28.

6   'Jiang Endorses Internet, with Some Limitations', Chicago Tribune, 22 August 2000.

7   World Bank and Development Research Center of the State Council, China 2030: Building a Modern, Harmonious, and Creative Society (Washington DC: World Bank, 2013), http://www.worldbank.org/content/dam/Worldbank/document/China-2030-complete.pdf.

8   Kathrin Hille, 'Chinese Communist Party Opens Online Forum', Financial Times, 14 September 2010.

9   Organisation for Economic Cooperation and Development, OECD Information Technology Outlook 2006 (OECD, 2006), p. 141.

10 Helen H. Wang, 'How eBay Failed in China', Forbes, 13 September 2010.

11 'The Internet in China', Information Office of the State Council, 8 June 2010, http://news.xinhuanet.com/english2010/china/2010-06/08/c_13339232.htm.

12 'China Cracks Down on Virtual Currency, for Real', Wall Street Journal, 29 June 2009.

13 'Guofang shengjie wan wangluo youxi zhangwo zhanshu zhishi', PLA Daily, 6 April 2010, http://news.xinhuanet.com/mil/2010-04/06/content_13307478.htm.

14 Geoffrey A. Fowler and Joanna Stern, 'Why We're Jealous of Chinese Smartphones', Wall Street Journal, 18 August 2015.

15 'China E-Commerce Market Rises 21.3% in 2014', iResearch, 17 February 2015.

16 Austin, Cyber Policy in China, p. 89.

17 Organisation for Economic Cooperation and Development, China in the World Economy: The Domestic Policy Challenges (OECD, 2002), p. 789.

18 Austin, Cyber Policy in China, p. 117.

19 Ibid., p. 113.

20 Adam Segal, 'China's Innovation Wall', Foreign Affairs, 28 September 2010.

21 Michael Kan, 'Windows XP Will Continue Receiving Security

Support in China', PC World, 3 March 2014.

22 'Wangluo kongjian baowei zhan', Economic National News Network, 4 August 2014, http://tech.163.com/14/0804/11/A2Q615RN000915BF.html.

23 Ministry of Public Security, 'Computer Information Network and Internet Security, Protection and Management Regulations – 1997', 1997, http://www.lehmanlaw.com/resource-centre/laws-and-regulations/information-technology/computer-information-network-and-internet-security-protection-and-management-regulations-1997.html.

24 Miguel Helft and David Barboza, 'Google Shuts China Site in Dispute Over Censorship', New York Times, 22 March 2010.

25 'China's "Brother Watch" Sentenced to 14 Years in Prison', Daily Telegraph, 5 September 2013.

26 John Chan, 'Anti-Japanese Protests Erupt in China', World Socialist Web Site, 8 April 2005.

27 'Clinton Says Trade Deal and Internet Will Reform China', Tech Law Journal, 9 March 2000.

28 'China Employs Two Million Microblog Monitors State Media Say', BBC, 4 October 2013.

29 Tao Zhu et al., 'The Velocity Of Censorship: High-Fidelity Detection of Microblog Post Deletions', 22nd USENIX Security Symposium, August 2013.

30 Gary King, Jennifer Pan and Margaret E. Roberts, 'Reverse-engineering Censorship in China: Randomized Experimentation and Participant Observation', Science, vol. 345, no. 6199, August 2014.

31 Kentaro Toyama, 'How Internet Censorship Actually Works in China', Atlantic, 2 October 2013.

32 US–China Economic and Security Review Commission, '2010 Report to Congress', November 2010, pp. 222–3, http://origin.www.uscc.gov/sites/default/files/annual_reports/2010-Report-to-Congress.pdf.

33 'Bo Xilai Scandal: Timeline', BBC, 11 November 2013.

34 Willy Lam, 'Xi Jinping's Ideological Crackdown Could Destroy China's Economy', AsiaNews.it, 10 April 2013.

35 'Build Our Country from a Large Internet Country into a Strong Internet Country', Xinhua, 27 February 2014.

36 'Zhongyang wangluo anquan he xinxihua lingdao xiaozu chengyuan mingdan 12 zhengfu guoji jianzhi shengaizu', Guancha, 28 February 2014, http://www.guancha.cn/politics/2014_02_28_209672.shtml.

37 'China Debates Constitutional Government', Voice of America, 3 June 2013.

38 Chris Buckley, 'China Takes Aim at Western Ideas', New York Times, 19 August 2013.

39 Rogier Creemers, 'Cyber China: Upgrading Propaganda, Public Opinion Work and Social Management for the 21st Century', Journal of Contemporary China, forthcoming, available at http://papers.ssrn.com/sol3/papers.cfm?abstract_id=2698062.

40 'Cyber Criminals Target China's Huge Online Population', China Times, 1 September 2015.

41 National People's Congress Standing Committee, 'Guanyu jiaqiang wangluo xinxi baohu de jueding', 28 December 2012,

https://chinacopyrightandmedia.
wordpress.com/2012/12/28/
national-peoples-congress-
standing-committee-decision-
concerning-strengthening-network-
information-protection/.

42 'Renmin wangping: yi fa zhi guo
rang fazhi zhongguo geng you
dise', *People's Daily*, 28 August
2014, http://opinion.people.com.cn/
n/2014/1027/c1003-25917653.html.

43 'Lu Wei Lays Out Four Rules for
Being a "Good Netizen"', *China
Digital Times*, 12 June 2015.

44 'China Unveils "Internet Plus"
Action Plan to Fuel Growth',
Xinhua, 4 July 2015.

45 King & Wood Mallesons, 'China
Banking IT Regulations Tightened
Up', China Law Insight, 16 March
2015.

46 Timothy P. Stratford and Yan Luo,
'China's New National Security
Law', *National Law Review*, 7 July
2015.

47 China Law Translate,
'Cybersecurity Law (Draft)', 6 July
2015, http://chinalawtranslate.com/
cybersecuritydraft/?lang=en.

48 Private communication, March
2015.

49 Michael Kan, 'China: Facebook
not Banned, but Must Follow the
Rules', PC World, 30 October 2014.

CHAPTER TWO

Cyber Espionage

Intelligence has played a central role in Chinese policy and strategy since the era of the Warring States (circa 475–221 BCE), a period in which Sunzi published *Sunzi Bingfa* (*Art of War*), devoting an entire chapter of the book to the subject. Espionage has also featured in classical literature such as *Sanguo Yanyi* (*Romance of Three Kingdoms*), which includes archetypal intelligence and deception operations such as Zhuge Liang's empty-city strategy. And espionage undoubtedly shaped the efforts of successive Chinese dynasties to manage relations with what they called the 'barbarian' nomadic tribes, as part of a border-management strategy that was for most of China's history the extent of its foreign policy. Due to this tendency to look inwards, the practice of foreign-intelligence collection (as it is understood in the West) was not a major feature of China's intelligence culture until comparatively recently.

Intelligence was important in the 1937–45 Sino-Japanese War and the 1945–49 civil war between Mao Zedong's Chinese Communist Party (CCP) and Chiang Kai-shek's Kuomintang. The communists had some significant intelligence successes in both conflicts: during the former, they acquired in 1941 predictive information on Adolf Hitler's invasion of the Soviet Union and Japan's military expansion into the Pacific; during the latter, they achieved comprehensive penetration of the intelligence organs of a demoralised Kuomintang.[1] The events of this era continue to define the image of espionage in Chinese popular culture, through novels such as the *Knifepoint* series by Mai Jia, an officer in the People's Liberation Army (PLA), and countless films and TV programmes – a trend encouraged by the CCP as part of its Patriotic Education Programme.[2] But the overwhelming majority of this intelligence was generated from within China, and the country had only a limited capacity to collect useful intelligence overseas.

Following the establishment of the People's Republic in 1949, China's intelligence community was largely focused on combating perceived security threats from a variety of domestic anti-communist groups, and had little scope to engage in foreign collection. Excepting the Soviet Union, then a close ally, China's external environment was largely hostile, with the West perceiving Chinese communist subversion in Asia as a significant international threat. Apart from formal diplomatic relations conducted through the Ministry of Foreign Affairs, such external engagement as China had took the form of interaction with fraternal communist parties via the CCP's International Liaison Department, as well as the cultivation of links with diaspora communities and foreign sympathisers (a task undertaken by the CCP's United Front Work Department). Capabilities in foreign-intelligence collection were constrained by a bunker mentality, as well as problems of access: China's intelligence officers had limited options for overseas deployments, were conspicuous and hence easily kept under surveillance, and were primarily reliant on ethnic-Chinese sources, few of whom had high-level access in Western countries.

The organisation responsible for foreign-intelligence collection was a Party organ – the Social Affairs Department until 1955, and thereafter the *diaochabu* (Investigation Department of the Central Committee of the CCP, or ID/CCP). Counter-intelligence and counter-espionage operations were carried out by a state entity, the *gonganbu* (Ministry of Public Security, or MPS). Much of the ID/CCP's work focused on dealing with ideological heterodoxy within the Party, and foreign-intelligence collection was in the main run by the MPS. Such foreign operations included those of Larry Wu-Tai Chin, a young interpreter whom the CCP infiltrated into US government service in China before the establishment of the People's Republic. He went on to join the CIA-controlled Foreign Broadcast Information Service, and provided his MPS case officers with a stream of high-grade intelligence on Sino-American relations and related topics, until his retirement in 1981 (he was unmasked by a defector in 1985, and committed suicide before being brought to trial).[3] And, in the early 1960s, there was the bizarre case of Bernard Boursicot, a young French diplomat stationed in Beijing, who was recruited by Chinese intelligence agents through his relationship with the transgender opera star Shi Peipu – a case that formed the basis of the modern play and film *M. Butterfly*. But these were exceptions during a period in which China became increasingly isolated and self-absorbed, culminating in the anarchy and institutional degradation of the 1966–76 Cultural Revolution, during which the country's foreign-intelligence activities all but ceased.[4]

The slow restoration of normality after 1976 coincided with a gradual opening up to the outside world, which had begun with US President Richard Nixon's 1972 visit to Beijing and the establishment of a Sino-American alliance against the Soviet Union. One consequence of this opening up was the establishment in 1980 of two US-owned, Chinese-operated signals-intelligence (SIGINT) stations at Qitai and Korla, in Xinjiang. The purpose of these stations, which continued operating until the end of the Cold War, was to monitor and collect telemetry data on Soviet missile and nuclear-weapons tests, as well as space launches.[5] With the initiation in 1979 of Deng Xiaoping's reform and opening-up programme, China began a frantic race to make up for decades of Maoist obscurantism in which ideological conformity – 'redness' – was prized over any form of technical expertise. Select foreign companies were invited to set up assembly lines in China, and small numbers of Chinese students began to attend Western academic institutions. This period saw the beginnings of a major, broad-spectrum overt and covert collection effort aimed at bridging the gap between China and the developed world. The undertaking has continued into the twenty-first century, and it lies at the heart – though does not encompass the totality – of the country's programme of foreign-intelligence collection.

China's intelligence structures

In 1983 the newly created *guojia anquanbu* (Ministry of State Security, or MSS) replaced the ID/CCP. The MSS combined the external-collection functions of the ID/CCP with the counter-intelligence and counter-espionage functions of the MPS, which in turn became a public-order and policing organisation. Despite its foreign-collection responsibilities, the MSS has always primarily focused on preserving domestic stability. Li Fengzhi, a member of the MSS until his defection to the US, has characterised its role as being to 'control the Chinese people to maintain the power of the Chinese Communist Party'.[6] Accordingly, most of the organisation's efforts at home and abroad are designed to counter what the CCP calls the 'Three Evil Forces' of separatism, terrorism and religious extremism, all of which are existential threats to Party rule.[7]

An organogram of the MSS resembles that of most modern intelligence organisations. It comprises a First Bureau with overall responsibility for overseas collection, using a wide range of non-official cover officers and casual sources such as students, academics and businessmen engaged in short-term overseas travel; and a Second Bureau responsible for overseas collection via legal residencies – a recent innovation, since Deng banned MSS officers from taking up cover posts in diplomatic missions – and officers using quasi-official cover as journalists for newspapers such as *Guangming Daily*. The MSS also has bureaux responsible for collection against domestic targets, counter-intelligence, counter-espionage and technical collection, as well as surveillance and intelligence analysis. Like many Chinese ministries, the MSS has its own think tank, the China Institutes of Contemporary International Relations, an entity that long predates the formation of the MSS, and that combines analytical functions with a range of para-diplomatic engagements. Most of the actual foreign-intelligence collection within the MSS is conducted by the State Security Bureaux (SSBs). The Shanghai SSB carries out collection against the United States and its main Western allies; the neighbouring Zhejiang SSB against Northern Europe; the Qingdao SSB against Japan and the Koreas; the Guangzhou SSB against Hong Kong, Taiwan and Southeast Asia; and the Beijing SSB against Eastern Europe and Russia. Foreign SIGINT collection appears to be organised along broadly similar geographical lines.

Since its formation, the MSS has occupied a somewhat uncertain position between its responsibilities for internal and external activities. A key driver behind the creation of the organisation was Deng's determination to ensure that the primary Chinese intelligence agency would never again become politicised or involved in Party matters – in the manner that the ID/CCP had during the Cultural Revolution, under the leadership of Kang Sheng.[8] In that period, the ID/CCP had persecuted Mao's opponents within the Chinese leadership, including Deng and members of his family.[9] The overseas work of the MSS has focused on collection against subversive groups, and it is possible that – as contended by Falun Gong, a pseudo-religious cult that is one of its primary targets – the agency was China's first to appreciate the potential of cyber capabilities in such activity.[10] The MSS has always appeared to be a relatively technocratic organisation, somewhat distanced from the internal political manoeuvring and institutional corruption that have long featured in China's domestic politics.

However, that appeared to change in 2007, when Zhou Yongkang became secretary of the Central Political and Legal Affairs Committee, the top-level Party organ responsible for, inter alia, oversight of China's police, judiciary and domestic intelligence services, including the MSS. Having begun his career in the oil and gas sector, and having served as minister of public security, Zhou established himself as a pivotal figure in the *shiyoubang* (oil and gas mafia).[11] Due to the importance of energy supplies to China's economic development, the *shiyoubang* became one of the powerful vested interests that took root under the leadership of Jiang Zemin and then Hu Jintao. The CCP saw such groups collectively as a major barrier to the implementation of the economic reforms needed to move China's economy away from an export-led model and thereby avoid the middle-income trap. Zhou's arrest on corruption charges – which came shortly after the spectacular fall from grace of his ally Bo Xilai, former Party chief of Chongqing – was a remarkable departure from the tradition of China's top leaders enjoying immunity from prosecution. And there are indications that Zhou was unwilling to come quietly: around the time of his arrest, there were rumours of a possible coup, and even of assassination attempts against both Hu and his successor, Xi Jinping.[12] The MSS appeared to have become a part of Zhou's patronage network and, after the investigation into his activities began, the organisation suffered several embarrassments. The first of these came in 2012, when MSS Vice-Minister Lu Zhongwei was forced into early retirement after it was discovered that his secretary was a long-time CIA agent.[13] In January 2015, Ma Jian, another MSS vice-minister, was caught up in the anti-corruption drive Xi launched in 2013, shortly after taking office; later the same year, Qiu Jin, also an MSS vice-minister, was arrested for allegedly instructing the head of the Beijing SSB to monitor the communications of senior Chinese leaders.[14]

Some Western analysts suggest that the MSS will be repositioned to focus on foreign-intelligence collection,[15] as the MPS – which is responsible for domestic cyber security and operates an advanced network of technical-surveillance capabilities – increasingly takes the lead in domestic security.[16] Indeed, the MPS has largely taken charge of the operation to track down officials who have fled overseas with embezzled state funds, nicknamed the 'fox hunt'.[17] The agency's use of undercover operatives to target these officials in the US and other countries has prompted official protests from the states concerned,[18] a fact that suggests the organisation has little experience of such overseas efforts and hence the international political sensibilities involved. Nonetheless, Chen Wenqing's appointment as MSS Party secretary, a post that gives him a seat on the Central Committee, may indicate that the agency will continue to have a strong domestic focus. This is because Chen – putatively the successor to Minister Geng Huichang – has a background in domestic security and law enforcement, and his previous role was in the Central Commission for Discipline Inspection.[19]

China's military also has significant capabilities for collecting foreign intelligence, situated in the *zongcan erbu* and the *zongcan sanbu* (Second and Third departments of the PLA General Staff, or 2/PLA and 3/PLA respectively). The former is primarily visible through its global network of defence attachés, who are all cadre 2/PLA officers selected mainly on the basis of their analytical capabilities and language skills, and who have little, if any, conventional military training or experience. This network has focused on collecting and analysing open-source information, and does not appear to engage in covert collection operations out of legal residencies.[20] However, their work is supplemented by a significant covert operation involving non-official cover officers, who have had some major successes – particularly in collecting information on high-end Western weapons systems such as the B-1 bomber, the B-2 stealth bomber, the Quiet Electric Drive submarine-propulsion system and the W-88 miniaturised nuclear warhead.[21] Some of the PLA operatives involved in this technology theft were planted in the US on a long-term basis. One such operative is Chi Mak, who was sentenced in April 2008 to 24 years in prison for stealing the designs of advanced US military systems manufactured by his employers. Chi admitted that he had been infiltrated into the US 20 years prior to his arrest, with a remit to work himself into a position of access.[22] For most of the 1990s and the 2000s, 2/PLA was responsible for the majority of the scientific and technical espionage directed against the US and its main allies, and it was generally regarded as having better capabilities for collecting foreign intelligence than the MSS.

In contrast, 3/PLA is China's SIGINT agency. Until the advent of the internet, 3/PLA was a conventional military SIGINT agency, operating various collection platforms within China and, since the early 1990s, a gradually expanding chain of stations along the coast of Myanmar. These include a substantial facility at Great Coco Island in the Andaman Sea, which targets Indian naval capabilities,[23] as well as stations established in 1998 in Bejucal and Santiago de Cuba, which are directed towards US telecommunications and military-satellite communications.[24] The agency also operated embassy-based SIGINT facilities in Ankara and Baghdad during the First Gulf War, and in Belgrade during the Kosovo conflict.[25] In addition, 3/PLA has a variety of airborne and ship-based collection capabilities. There have been signs that 3/PLA has sought to extend its reach through joint operations with other states; one of these is Indonesia, which has reportedly used Chinese-supplied equipment to monitor Australian telecommunications, and has shared the information collected with Beijing.[26] As is the case with the MSS and 2/PLA, there is no publicly available data on 3/PLA's organisational structure, budget or staffing. But, according to one Western scholar,

> The PLA's SIGINT community consists of at least 28 technical reconnaissance bureaus (TRBs) … It has direct authority over 12 operational bureaus, three research institutes, and a computing center. Eight of the 12 operational bureau headquarters are clustered in Beijing. Two others are based in Shanghai, one in Qingdao, and one in Wuhan. Ten additional TRBs provide direct support to the PLA's seven military regions (MRs), while another six support the PLA Navy (PLAN), Air Force (PLAAF), and Second Artillery Force (PLASAF).[27]

Although modern information and communications technologies (ICTs) have transformed 3/PLA's capabilities, they have also brought the organisation an unwelcome degree of public attention, particularly in relation to the Shanghai-based PLA Unit 61398, which has conducted much of China's cyber industrial espionage against US corporations.

Intelligence tradecraft

Countries' intelligence services differ little in structure. What separates them is operational culture and ethos, together with factors such as the prestige accorded to intelligence work within a particular political culture. Another determinant of performance is the degree to which an intelligence service is integrated into the policymaking process of the state it purports to serve, and its perception of its influence on that process. China's intelligence agencies appear to have relatively limited political influence – the MSS, for example, is not regarded as a power ministry – nor does intelligence work appear to attract top-tier graduates as it does in the Anglo-Saxon political culture. But, by the same token, China's intelligence services do not seem to follow an agenda separate from that of the state, nor to have been greatly affected by corruption (the inclusion of the MSS in Zhou Yongkang's patronage network notwithstanding). While their recent achievements in scientific and technical collection are significant, it is much harder to judge accurately their effectiveness in collecting political intelligence. Nonetheless, it is safe to say that their modus operandi in foreign-intelligence collection has evolved away from great caution and towards a self-confidence commensurate with China's rising status and influence in the world.

An important driver of these collection efforts has been the desire to catch up with the developed world in transformative science and technology. Launched in 1986, Plan 863 brought together Beijing's foreign-intelligence requirements in the areas of science and technology it saw as crucial to China's economic development. The plan had originally centred on a research and development programme proposed to Deng by a group of nuclear-weapons scientists, but it quickly morphed into a more general project designed to eliminate Chinese dependence on strategically important foreign technologies.[28] The impetus to pursue the covert foreign-collection element of Plan 863 grew rapidly during the 1991 First Gulf War, spurred by the PLA's shock at the scope and complexity of US precision weaponry deployed against the forces of Iraqi President Saddam Hussein. Advanced US military systems subsequently became a priority target, and accordingly the Chinese intelligence services – primarily 2/PLA – exploited a unique asset: ethnic-Chinese nationals working in some of the most highly classified US military programmes. There seems little doubt that information on these programmes was transferred to China, which was able to reverse-engineer the relevant systems. However, efforts by the US Department of Justice to prosecute ethnic-Chinese scientists who worked on these programmes and were suspected of having passed information to China have been notably unsuccessful. A case in point is that of Wen Ho Lee, a physicist at Los Alamos National Laboratory whom the Department of Justice accused of having passed to China details on technology relating to the W-88 miniaturised nuclear warhead. After being indicted by a federal grand jury on 59 counts of mishandling classified information, Lee was detained in solitary confinement for nine months, before a plea bargain led him to plead guilty on one count. Having received an apology from the judge for his harsh treatment, Lee left court a free man.[29]

Apart from the high-profile cases such as that cited above, much Chinese scientific and technical collection was, and continues to be, undertaken at a level just below the radar. This is done either by Chinese academics and businessmen travelling abroad, who pick up individual pieces of information that are not in themselves especially sensitive or compromising, or by Chinese specialists in the respective disciplines skilfully picking the brains of Western scientists visiting China. Following generous – and tiring – Chinese hospitality, the latter could often be persuaded to reveal details about their work. Dave Szady, former FBI head of counter-intelligence, characterised such practices as forming the 'thousand grains of sand approach', and they feature in a book written in 1991 by two Chinese intelligence officers, whose central thesis is that the majority of intelligence requirements can be met through the accumulation of open-source material. China's intelligence-collection efforts have also leveraged the connections it established through sales involving state-owned defence corporations, such as Norinco and Poly Technologies. As time has gone by, the country's top-level covert scientific and technical collection has become progressively more focused and professional, even as the noise of low-grade acquisitions has continued.[30]

China's intelligence services have proven particularly adept at exploiting the ambiguities in US legislation on espionage and the transmission of classified materials – the latter not a criminal offence in itself. As a result, US investigations into spying have often failed to come to trial or have resulted in token sentences on unrelated charges, as was allegedly the case with MSS/FBI double agent Katrina Leung.[31] And China's intelligence agencies appear to have abandoned their reservations about recruiting non-Chinese assets, as evidenced by the cases of US nationals Noshir Gowadia,[32] Glenn Duffie Shriver[33] and James Wilbur Fondren Jr,[34] as well as that of Russian physicist Valentin Danilov. (Danilov was paroled in November 2012 after serving ten years of a 14-year sentence for selling Russian satellite technology to a Chinese corporation.[35])

There is also growing evidence that China's intelligence services are willing to conduct operations against foreign nationals outside the country, and to be more adventurous in their undertakings abroad. In 2008 an MSS officer was discovered to have recruited a Uighur émigré to report on the activities of Sweden's Uighur population. In 2009 the German authorities uncovered a Chinese espionage network in Munich run by an MSS officer based in the Chinese consulate there.[36] And, in 2011, the Chinese intelligence services recruited the Taiwanese army's director of telecommunications and electronic information in Bangkok.[37] Meanwhile, China's operations against foreign targets have become more widespread and blatant, and in some cases more intimidatory. In 2005 a diplomat in the Japanese consulate in Shanghai committed suicide following what was described as an attempt at blackmail involving a Shanghai SSB honey trap.[38] In 2008 an aide to British Prime Minister Gordon Brown found that his mobile phone was missing after he had spent the night with a young Chinese girl he had met in a Shanghai discotheque.[39] In 2015 an Australian-Chinese businessman went public with a complaint that, after he had rejected an approach from the MSS, members of his family in China were arrested, his business forced to close, and he and his family subjected to intimidation and surveillance in Australia.[40]

CCP policy on intelligence

China has no central machinery for assessing intelligence and putting out analyses that reflect an agreed government position – of the kind produced by the US National Intelligence Council, the Australian Office of National Assessments or the UK Joint Intelligence Committee. The country's nearest equivalent is a Party organ, the Foreign Affairs Office of the Central Committee's Bureau of Policy Research, which does not put out analyses of its own but rather assesses reports by government agencies and think tanks, and provides commentary and requests for clarifications or supplementary information.[41] (The General Office of the CCP Central Committee is responsible for distributing reports to leaders and government agencies, but it has no influence on the content of these reports.)

It was not until November 2013 that China established a mechanism comparable to the US or UK national-security committees, following the conclusion of the Third Plenum of the 18th CCP Central Committee. Presidents Jiang and Hu had reportedly made efforts to establish such an organisation, but were unable to overcome entrenched individual and departmental reluctance to share power.[42] The Chinese mechanism for coordinating top-level policy has been the leading small group (LSG), which is used to address a range of strategic issues, both foreign and domestic. These LSGs operate throughout the Chinese system, with a top tier of them – ten under Hu and 11 under Xi – responsible for the formulation of national policy. China's state media outlets have published no comprehensive reporting on the composition, role and functions of the LSGs,[43] although some partial accounts have appeared since 2013. The role of the groups has also evolved. Under previous iterations of the central leadership, the LSGs were designed to bring together senior policymakers to debate, provide advice and issue recommendations on major policy issues for China's ultimate decision-making body, the Politburo Standing Committee (consisting of nine leaders until 2012, and seven since then). Working in that mode, the LSGs had little by way of executive capacity. In the words of one Chinese academic,

> As an informal and ad-hoc committee the [National Security LSG] does not operate as the core national security team designated to follow, analyze and co-ordinate daily national security ... In reality, its role is more or less confined to the organizer of research and coordinator [sic] of policies.[44]

However, since taking office, Xi has sought to strengthen Party control of the LSG system, and to use it to push forward his assertive, extrovert foreign-policy and security agenda. As described by one Western expert, LSGs now

> serve the policymaking process in two ways – policy formulation and policy implementation. With regard to the former role, once the leadership initiates the poli- cymaking process, the relevant leading small group and its general office manage the preparatory work of enlisting the collaboration among relevant [Central Committee] departments, State Council ministries and agencies, components of the Chinese People's Political Consultative Conference, and other institutions, orga- nizing relevant inspection work, and soliciting expert recommendations. The group then drafts a report for the leadership and formulates policy proposals to prepare for a final decision by the leadership. The leading small group's role in this process is critical in ironing out a consensus on the policy issue among competing and clashing views among the collaborating institutions.[45]

According to Zhou Wang, lecturer at Nankai University, 'because the presiding member of the leading small group is also a principal member of the leadership collective, the policy proposals that the leading small group formulates will all essentially be adopted'.[46] The LSGs are served by *bangongshi* (permanent offices), which provide administrative support, conduct research, prepare policy options for discussion and play a coordinating role. As evidenced by the actions of Lu Wei – director of the Cyberspace Administration of China, the *bangongshi* for the LSG for Cybersecurity and Informatization – the heads of these entities have considerable power.

The ways in which intelligence shapes this process remain unclear, as does the weight given to the product from China's intelligence services relative to information such as that provided by the Ministry of Foreign Affairs, other ministries, state-owned enterprises and open-source material. Since China's intelligence community began sustained, systematic cyber collection, there has in principle been an exponential growth in the quantity of foreign intelligence available to the country's leaders. Yet there is some doubt about how well they assess such intelligence. It may be that China's intelligence community suffers from the same problem as that of the Soviet Union: the need to pass information through an ideological filter in a way that diminishes its utility and impact. As any intelligence officer knows, such information vies with a range of other material for the attention of policymakers, and China's leaders are far from unique in drawing on their own sources. The use of scientific and technical intelligence is more straight-forward, as this material will be made available to whichever research institute is best placed to exploit it for commercial purposes.

Deployment of intelligence cyber capabilities

Much has been written in China on the subject of cyber warfare. By contrast, there is little discussion in the country of cyber exploitation, or cyber espionage – apart from a succes-sion of official denials that China engages in, and assertions that it is the victim of, such activity. But the phenomenon is of great strategic concern to Western policymakers. Since the turn of the twenty-first century, there has been a massive growth in cyber-exploitation operations apparently emanating from China, which have targeted the classified systems of govern-ments and major corporations, as well as groups that oppose the Chinese government, such as Falun Gong. The list of such attacks is long (see Table 2.1 for the most significant and widely reported among them).

China has been the staging area for not only a series of high-end attacks, but also many less advanced exploitation operations, characterised by those on the receiving end as noisy and reduplicative. Many of the high-end attacks have been significant less in their technological complexity than in the imagination they involve, with their perpetrators approaching targets from unexpected angles. Moreover, as Dmitri Alperovitch observed in his investigation into *Operation Shady Rat* (see Table 2.1), even the more advanced attacks showed some surprising lapses in tradecraft. These included a cycle of activities that coincided with the rhythms of the Chinese working day, a suspension of activities on Chinese public holidays and the use of Chinese coding language and IP addresses.[47] None of these facts are incontrovertible evidence of Chinese-state involvement: as has been argued, other actors may have taken advantage of the country's notoriously insecure ICT networks and dependence on pirated (and hence insecure) software to launch springboard attacks via Chinese servers. However, if one acknowledges that the targets of the high-end attacks align with the priorities of the CCP's successive Five-Year Plans[48] and simply asks 'cui bono?', it is hard to reach any other conclusion than that their perpetrators were acting in the perceived interests of Beijing.

Yet, as was true of China's scientific and technical intelligence collection before the Internet Age, not all of the country's cyber espionage is being undertaken by entities that are formally part of the state. This fact may have enabled China's top leadership to issue public denials that the state is engaged in commercial espionage. Such activity involves many other organisations, most of which are best described as 'partial state actors' or, to borrow a term from an earlier era, 'privateers': groups of hackers co-opted by the state or employed by state-owned or private companies to steal intellectual property. The arrival of the internet in China allowed for the emergence of numerous groups of indigenous hackers, some of the best-known of which are the China Hacker Union and the *hongke* (Honker Union). As Scott Henderson explains in his book *The Dark Visitor*, 'such entities operate quite openly on the Internet, maintaining their own Web pages, recruiting new members and boasting of their hacking exploits ... These groups have generally been tolerated by the Chinese government as long as their hacking activities were directed abroad.'[49] And not just tolerated. In 2007–08 the MPS placed job advertisements on the websites of hacker groups XFocus and EvilOctal. Moreover, the PLA has reportedly organised hacking competitions, adver-

Table 2.1: **Cyber espionage linked with China**

2003	A series of intrusions are conducted into US government and contractor networks, collectively referred to by the code name *Titan Rain*.[50]
2006–07	The governments of the United Kingdom, Germany and New Zealand publicise details of cyber attacks allegedly emanating from China. The director-general of the UK Security Service takes the unprecedented step of writing a letter to 300 chief executives and security advisers in private corporations, alerting them to the threat of cyber exploitation by China.[51]
2009	The Information Warfare Monitor, run by the Citizen Lab at the University of Toronto's Munk School, releases a report on the so-called *Ghost Net* attack against the computer systems of the Dalai Lama, ultimately infecting 1,200 computers in 103 countries.[52] Details emerge about an attack on the networks of US oil and gas corporations, including Marathon, ExxonMobil and ConocoPhillips. The primary aim of these exploitation operations, collectively referred to as *Night Dragon*, is to collect data on the quantity, value and location of oil deposits worldwide.[53]
2010	Google is targeted in an advanced hacking operation code-named *Aurora*. The incident follows the company's decision to move its Chinese base of operations to Hong Kong, after its reluctance to impose Chinese-mandated censorship criteria leads to increasingly fraught relations with Beijing. *Aurora* appears to be designed to access Google's source code, as a prelude to accessing the systems of other US corporations. The attack also targets Adobe, Dow Chemical and Northrop Grumman, whose proprietary data is found by Google investigators on a server in Taiwan used for the intrusions. The Gmail accounts of Chinese dissidents are also targeted. The FBI subsequently reveals that one aim of the intrusion is to determine whether the Gmail accounts of Chinese non-official cover officers operating in the US are being monitored by American authorities.[54]
2011	McAfee publishes the results of an investigation, entitled *Shady Rat*, into multiple cyber intrusions conducted over the preceding five years. The operations targeted the networks of governments, private companies and international organisations, including the United Nations and the International Olympic Committee.[55]
2012	General Keith Alexander, director of the National Security Agency and head of Cyber Command, confirms to the US Senate that China was behind an attack the previous year on the RSA SecurID two-factor security authentication system, used by contractors engaged in classified work for the Pentagon.[56]

tising the events in local newspapers and offering large cash prizes, with the aim of recruiting the winners in cyber militias.[57] The activities of such militias have been supplemented by those of patriotic hacker groups, which participated in the Sino-American hacker war of 2001 – a week-long series of attacks and counter-attacks sparked by Washington's resumption of arms sales to Taiwan and US airborne surveillance off the Chinese coast.[58]

Since those early days, China's hackers have tended to move in one of two directions, either transforming themselves into legitimate cyber-security companies, as has been the case with XFocus.com, or going to the dark side and becoming involved in the kinds of cyber criminality that are increasingly lucrative

Table 2.1: **Cyber espionage linked with China (continued)**

2013	US security company Mandiant produces a report on the activities of PLA Unit 61398, which is described as having extracted hundreds of terabytes of data from more than 140 organisations.[59]
	The US Defense Science Board publishes a report for the Pentagon stating that the designs for more than 20 advanced US weapons systems have been compromised. These included the PAC-3 *Patriot* missile; the *Aegis* system for ballistic-missile defence; the US Army's Terminal High Altitude Area Defence system; the F/A-18 *Super Hornet* fighter jet; the V-22 *Osprey* tilt-rotor aircraft; the UH-60 *Black Hawk* helicopter; the F-35 Joint Strike Fighter; and the US Navy's littoral combat ship. The report does not ascribe this espionage to China, but senior military and civilian officials indicate that the bulk of this activity forms part of a widening campaign of Chinese spying on US defence contractors and government agencies.[60]
2014	The US Department of Justice unseals indictments against five named PLA officers associated with PLA Unit 61398.[61]
	US-based organisation Novetta publishes a report, entitled 'Operation SMN: Axiom Threat Actor Group Report', detailing the activities of what it describes as a 'well resourced, disciplined and sophisticated' cyber espionage group operating out of mainland China. This group had operated undetected for up to six years, targeting non-governmental organisations and other civil-society groups viewed as hostile by the Chinese government. The group also targeted 'organizations that are of strategic economic interest, that influence environmental and energy policy, and that develop cutting edge information technology including integrated circuits, telecommunications equipment manufacturers and infrastructure providers'.[62]
2015	The US government announces that hackers have breached the databases of its Office of Personnel Management. The attack had resulted in the compromise of the personnel records of around 4.2 million federal employees. In a second breach, which had gone undetected for over a year, the records of a further 21.5m federal employees were compromised.[63] Washington does not publicly attribute the attack to China, but in private US officials express little doubt that the country is responsible, and that its intelligence services gained a wealth of targeting information.

within China. In the words of one Hong Kong journalist who has researched these groups,

> the individual hackers' pursuit of profit and personal gain has contributed to the decline of large amateur hacker groups in China. Today's hackers turn increasingly to profitable online crimes such as banking fraud or identity theft, and Beijing doesn't have strong and comprehensive laws to effectively stop these crimes.[64]

However, it is equally true that within China there remain many groups of hackers operating on behalf of the state or entities connected with the state, or engaging in opportunistic collection against foreign targets with the aim of selling the proceeds to the highest bidder. The latter practice also occurs within the official intelligence community, with some 3/PLA officers known to moonlight in collecting intelligence unrelated to their formal remit, for sale to private companies.[65] The overall picture is of widely dispersed activity lacking both adequate central control and a systematic risk–benefit calculus.

A 2009 report prepared by Northrop Grumman for the US–China Economic and Security Review Commission describes in detail some of the more advanced operations emanating from China that have targeted US government agencies and private-sector networks. Such operations appear to be the product of detailed, careful reconnaissance aimed at understanding the workings of the network under attack, as well as social and professional network analysis to find the most appropriate entry point. The latter is normally achieved through a 'spear-phishing' attack, which may be directed against individuals at several degrees of separation from the eventual target. (A 'spear-phishing' attack involves sending select individuals emails with attachments containing Trojan viruses, which when activated provide the attacker with remote access to the target network. In the most effective such operations, the emails are carefully designed to be consistent with those the intended target would expect to receive, to maximise the likelihood that they will be opened.) The Northrop Grumman report describes a division of labour between the breach team, tasked with gaining covert entry into the system, and the exploitation team, responsible for locating and exfiltrating data. It concludes that:

> The scale and complexity of targeting associated with this effort suggest that it is probably backed by a mature collection management bureaucracy able to collate and disseminate collection priorities to diverse teams of operators, intelligence analysts and malware developers. These individuals are likely a mix of uniformed officers, military personnel, civilian intelligence operatives and freelance high-end hackers.[66]

Both Western governments and other entities investigating episodes of cyber espionage were for many years cautious about unequivocally laying such activities at China's door – on the grounds that it is hard to determine the origins of some activity in the cyber domain, where messages can be routed through multiple transit points to disguise the identities of their senders. That changed in February 2013, when US-based cyber-security company Mandiant released a report on the activities of PLA Unit 61398. The Chinese government predictably denied the allegations in the document,[67] but shortly after its publication, the buildings identified by Mandiant appeared to have been vacated.[68] The report was the catalyst for a more direct approach by the US government, and at the Sunnylands summit between Xi and US President Barack Obama, held during 7–8 June 2013, the issue of cyber security was put at the top of the bilateral agenda – albeit without Xi giving any ground by acknowledging China's culpability.[69] One month later, there was the first meeting of the new cyber-security working group within the framework of the annual US–China Strategic and Economic Dialogue.[70] Xinhua, China's official news agency, described the discussion as having gone well,[71] but there was little evidence that the sides had made much progress. By that point, rogue National Security Agency contractor Edward Snowden had begun to make revelations about the extent of cyber espionage carried out by the US and its Five Eyes allies (Australia, Canada, New Zealand and the United Kingdom). Snowden's disclosures reinforced Chinese perceptions that the US was using its privileged position within the cyber domain to perpetuate American hegemony, and that Washington's accusations against Beijing reflected double standards.[72]

In making its case against China's state-sponsored cyber industrial espionage, the US government sought to distinguish between conventional state-on-state spying for the purposes of national security – an activity that is not proscribed by international law – and the theft of intellectual property. The US argued that China had breached its treaty commitments as a member of the World Trade Organisation, specifically in connection with the Trade-Related Aspects of Intellectual Property Rights (TRIPS), which oblige governments to protect intellectual property.[73] This interpretation of TRIPS was contentious in that, as Chinese experts on international law quickly pointed out, it was never conceived of as having an extraterritorial dimension.[74] Moreover, Chinese security officials privately made clear that, for China, economic development was an issue of national security, since the CCP's failure to achieve its economic goals might give rise to widespread social unrest, creating an existential threat to the regime.[75] In effect, these officials were saying that cyber industrial espionage was a quasi-legitimate way to achieve a North–South redistribution of wealth. This outlook reflected the pervasive, long-standing Chinese perception that, in the words of one Chinese commentator, 'the West forced on China an inequitable distribution of the benefits of science and technology … depriving China of its legitimate rights'.[76] Such claims are tendentious to say the least, although it is true that from 1950 until the mid-1980s trade, scientific and technical exchanges with China were severely restricted under a Coordinating Committee for Multilateral Export Controls regime that, while it was gradually relaxed in its latter years, only formally ended in 1994. And China remains subject to an arms embargo applied by the US and the European Union in the wake of the 1989 massacre in Tiananmen Square, even if this measure is largely symbolic.

Although many commentators accused the US government of failing to respond to China's cyber activities, Washington had begun to build a strategy that amounted to cross-domain retaliation. This strategy consisted of adopting a legal approach that sought to deal not with individual acts of cyber industrial espionage but rather the totality of the phenomenon, preparing legal action against Chinese corporations and individuals deemed to have benefited from stolen intellectual property. While such entities were once largely out of reach for US prosecutors, China's new policy of going out into the world has led to the former acquiring assets in jurisdictions in which legal action can be brought. This approach appeared to prompt four days of talks in Washington shortly before Xi's September 2015 state visit to the US, involving China's law-enforcement and intelligence agencies and their US counterparts – led by Secretary of the Politburo Central Political–Legal Committee Meng Jianzhu and Secretary for Homeland Security Jeh Johnson respectively.[77] It seems that the Chinese delegates at these meetings were apprised of Washington's intention to initiate legal proceedings against Chinese companies such as Chinalco Mining, China's largest aluminium company, Baosteel and State Nuclear Power Technology Corporation – all of which occupy a critical place in China's economy.[78] Such a threat might have had little impact several years earlier, but the fact that senior Chinese officials devoted so much time to the issue suggests that it concerned them. During Xi's trip, the US and Chinese governments announced an agreement under which they would not 'conduct or knowingly support cyber-enabled theft of intellectual property, including trade secrets or other confidential business information for commercial advantage'.[79] This statement is politically significant in that it represents a change in China's declaratory policy.

The US and China also announced during Xi's visit that they would establish a high-level joint dialogue on cyber crime – enabling officials from both countries to investigate allegations of cyber intrusions – as well as a hotline to deal with specific requests. The dialogue would be led on the US side by the secretary for homeland security and the attorney general, and on the Chinese side by the ministers of public and state security, as well as the Cyberspace Administration of China. The first meeting in the new dialogue took place in Washington on 1 December 2015. Xinhua reported that the participants

> identified a number of cases for future cooperation on enhancing cyber security, reached further consensus on fighting cyber terrorism, and agreed on some specific programs of strengthening capability building in fighting cyber crimes. Among the cases discussed included the one related to the alleged theft of data of the U.S. Office of Personnel Management by Chinese hackers. Through investigation, the case turned out to

be a criminal case rather than a state-sponsored cyber attack as the U.S. side has previously suspected.[80]

The final part of the statement is of particular interest, since it appears to represent a formal acknowledgement by China that the cyber operation originated in its territory. This is an intriguing assertion, not least because the attack was regarded by Washington as legitimate state espionage for national-security purposes – and had elicited reluctant admiration from the US intelligence community.

Global intelligence power

Shortly after Xi's September 2015 state visit, US officials let it be known that there had been a marked decline in commercial cyber-espionage operations conducted by the Chinese military since May the previous year, when the Department of Justice indicted five named officers in PLA Unit 61398 (see Table 2.1).[81] This trend may have partly resulted from the shock experienced by 3/PLA upon realising that US law-enforcement agencies had easily identified individual operatives. It may also have been connected with reforms of the PLA's command structure (see Chapter Three). One aspect of these could have involved a top-level decision to tighten up 3/PLA's online activities, including moonlighting in the private sector, and a refocusing of intelligence-collection efforts on defence-related targets.[82] Another possibility is that the Chinese leadership positioned the indictments as external pressure that justified a clean-up of China's domestic cyber environment, a process the CCP now recognises as critical to its ambitions for promoting the country's digital economy and integrating it into the wider economy. In line with this, there was a growing tide of arrests and prosecutions of cyber criminals within China in 2015.[83] It remains to be seen whether this activity will in aggregate lead to the taming of China's 'Wild East' and an improvement in the country's relationship with the US and its allies. A more likely scenario is that there will be a reduction in the relatively indiscriminate, noisy activity associated with low-end attacks, combined with a more advanced combination of cyber attacks and human-intelligence deployments against targets perceived to have good cyber security – and hence something valuable to protect. Indeed, law-enforcement and security officials in the US are already seeing evidence of such an approach.[84]

If 3/PLA has moved away from its earlier focus on commercial cyber espionage, it may be that the MSS, whose cyber operations appear to involve better tradecraft, will take up some of the slack. There is virtually no publicly available information on MSS cyber capabilities or the mechanisms for operational collaboration and deconfliction with 3/PLA. The MSS can certainly be expected to continue to monitor closely the online activities of dissidents based outside China. There are also indications that the MPS has moved into this arena, as suggested by the August 2015 'man-on-the-side' attack on GitHub, a US-based open-source code provider on which many Chinese citizens rely and which hosts GreatFire and the Chinese website of the *New York Times*. GreatFire provides tools enabling Chinese users to bypass the Golden Shield firewall, while the *New York Times* site has featured much disobliging reporting on issues such as the financial holdings of the families of Chinese leaders. The attack intercepted unencrypted requests directed from outside China to China's main search engine Baidu and injected pieces of JavaScript, flooding GitHub with access requests in a classic distributed denial-of-service operation. Furthermore, two Chinese-origin virtual private networks were pulled from the GitHub site, one of them reportedly at the direct insistence of the MPS.[85] This kind of extraterritorial censorship could well prove to be a defining feature of China's efforts to maintain control of content, although the high level of international attention generated by the episode could have a constraining effect.

As with so much else involving China, cyber espionage has led to a period of explosive activity – initially, with little in the way of top-level oversight and control – as the potential of new technology became apparent, driven by the overarching imperative of rapid economic and technological development, as well as a sense of grievance that the West has unfairly monopolised advanced scientific and technical knowledge. For most of the last decade, the risk–benefit calculus of commercial cyber espionage seemed entirely in China's favour. In effect, there was an asymmetry of vulnerability between China, which had an insatiable appetite for Western intellectual property, and Western countries, which focused on the collection of traditional forms of intelligence for the purposes of national security and statecraft. Yet it is difficult to measure the economic benefits China has derived from commercial cyber espionage, with both collectors and consumers of such material so widely distributed that there is no obvious pattern among them. The fact that exploits designed to collect information on one iteration of a technology are repeated against its subsequent versions suggests that, in many cases, China has failed to identify the underlying principles of that technology. The counterfactual question is: might China have done better to focus on genuine indigenous innovation rather than to devote so much energy to reverse-engineering Western technologies, many of which were heading towards obsolescence? Meanwhile, China's risk–benefit calculus appears to have shifted somewhat since the early years of the twenty-first century, towards greater discrimination and circumspection. It may be that the international furore over China's commercial espionage will be consigned to a footnote in history, as a period of growing pains that eventually passed

– much as happened with Japan in the 1960s and South Korea in the 1970s. But, in contrast to these latter states, China's intelligence culture has assimilated cyber capabilities in ways that make the country a formidable actor among the top tier of global intelligence powers. The question now is: what use will China make of these capabilities, and to what end?

Notes

1 David Ian Chambers, 'Edging in from the Cold: the Past and Present State of Chinese Intelligence Historiography', *Studies in Intelligence*, vol. 56, no. 3, September 2012.

2 See Zhao Suisheng, 'A State-Led Nationalism: The Patriotic Education Campaign in Post-Tiananmen China', *Communist and Post-Communist Studies*, vol. 31, no. 3, 1998, pp. 287–302.

3 'Espionage: A Spy's Grisly Solution', *Time*, 3 March 1986.

4 Chambers, 'Edging in from the Cold', p. 34.

5 Philip Taubman, 'US and Peking Join in Tracking Missiles in Soviet', *New York Times*, 18 June 1981.

6 Bill Gertz, 'Chinese Spy Who Defected Tells All', *Washington Times*, 19 March 2009.

7 Sam duPont, 'China's War on the "Three Evil Forces"', *Foreign Policy*, 25 July 2007.

8 Chambers, 'Edging in from the Cold', p. 34.

9 Peter Mattis, 'China's Intelligence Reforms?', *Diplomat*, 23 January 2013.

10 Joshua Philipp, 'How Silencing China's Dissidents Led to Stealing the West's Secrets', *Epoch Times*, 11 September 2015.

11 David Kan Ting, 'Pinning Hopes on Xi Jinping for Needed Reform in the PRC', *China Post*, 11 September 2013.

12 'Zhou Yongkang and his Failed Assassins', *China Uncensored*, 16 December 2013.

13 Peter Mattis, 'The Dragon's Eyes and Ears: Chinese Intelligence at the Crossroads', *National Interest*, 20 January 2015.

14 *Ibid.*

15 Peter Mattis, 'The Analytic Challenge of Understanding Chinese Intelligence Services', *Studies in Intelligence*, vol. 56, no. 3, September 2012, p. 52.

16 Peter Mattis, 'Informatization Drives Expanded Scope of Public Security', *China Brief*, vol. 13, no. 9, 12 April 2013.

17 'China's "Fox Hunt" Grabs 288 Officials in Worldwide Anti-Graft Net', Reuters, 17 November 2014.

18 Mark Mazzetti and Dan Levin, 'Obama Administration Warns Beijing about Covert Agents Operating in US', *New York Times*, 16 August 2015.

19 Peter Mattis, 'Chen Wenqing: China's New Man for State Security', *National Interest*, 23 October 2015.

20 William T. Hagestad II, *21st Century Chinese Cyberwarfare* (Cambridge: IT Governance, 2012), p. 16.

21 David Wise, 'China's Spies are Catching Up', *New York Times*, 10 December 2011.

22 Joby Warrick and Carrie Johnson, 'Chinese Spy "Slept" in US for 2 Decades', *Washington Post*, 3 April 2008.

23 'China is Potential Threat Number One', *Indian Express*, 4 May 1998.

24 Manuel Cereijo, 'China and Cuba and Information Warfare (IW): Signals Intelligence (SIGINT), Electronic Warfare (EW), and Cyber-Warfare', Cuban-American Military Council, http://www. camcocuba.org/ADDITIONAL%20 PAGES/CEREIJO%20E/CEREIJO-ENGLISH/CEREIJO-16-E.html.

25 Bradley Martin, 'China for Real: Embassy Bombing "Part of Espionage War"', *Asia Times*, 23 July 1999. While the claim in this article that China was collecting SIGINT in its Belgrade Embassy is almost certainly correct, the bombing of the Embassy by the US Air Force appears to have been an unfortunate accident.

26 Ian McPhedran, 'Indonesian Spies are Using Chinese Electronic Equipment to Spy on Aussies', News.com.au, 25 November 2013.

27 Mark A. Stokes, 'The PLA General Staff Department Third Department Second Bureau: An Organisational Overview of Unit 61398', Project 2049 Institute, 27 July 2015.

28 For a detailed account of the genesis and evolution of Plan 863, see Evan A. Feigenbaum, *China's Techno-warriors: National Security and Strategic Competition from the Nuclear to the Information Age* (Palo Alto, CA: Stanford University Press, 2000), pp. 141–66.

29 David Wise, *Tiger Trap: America's Secret Spy War with China* (Boston, MA: Houghton Mifflin Harcourt, 2011), pp. 81–98.

30 Nigel Inkster, 'The Chinese Intelligence Agencies: Evolution and Empowerment in Cyberspace', in Jon R. Lindsay, Tai Ming Cheung and Derek S. Reveron (eds), *China and Cybersecurity: Espionage, Strategy and Politics in the Digital Domain* (Oxford: Oxford University Press, 2015), p. 35.

31 Wise, *Tiger Trap*, pp. 1–5, 20–9, 109–21, 187–202.

32 Larkins Dsouza, 'Noshir Gowadia Father of Chinese Stealth Technology', *Defence Aviation*, 14 March 2012.

33 David Wise, 'Mole-in-Training: How China Tried to Infiltrate the CIA', *Washingtonian*, 7 June 2012.

34 'Pentagon Official Charged in Leak of Classified Info to China', CNN, 13 May 2009.

35 'Russia Paroles Physicist Valentin Danilov, Jailed for Spying', *Guardian*, 13 November 2012.

36 Holger Stark, 'Police Raid in Munich: Germany Suspects China of Spying on Uighur Expatriates', *Spiegel*, 24 November 2009.

37 Mattis, 'The Analytic Challenge of Understanding Chinese Intelligence Services'.

38 Justin McCurry, 'Japan Says Diplomat's Suicide Followed Blackmail by China', *Guardian*, 29 December 2005.

39 Andrew Porter, 'Downing Street Aide in Chinese "Honeytrap" Sting', *Daily Telegraph*, 20 July 2008.

40 'Beijing Intimidates Australian Citizen for Refusing to Spy', *China Digital Times*, 13 October 2015.

41 Yun Sun, 'Chinese National Security Decision-making: Processes and Challenges', Brookings Institution, May 2013.

42 Jean-Pierre Cabestan, 'China's Foreign- and Security-Policy Decision-Making Processes Under Hu Jintao', *Journal of Current Chinese Affairs*, vol. 38, no. 3, 2009, p. 66.

43 Kerry Dumbaugh and Michael F. Martin, 'Understanding China's Political System', Congressional Research Service, 31 December 2009, pp. 11–12.

44 Yun, 'Chinese National Security Decision-making'.

45 Alice L. Miller, 'More Already on the Central Committee's Leading Small Groups', *China Leadership Monitor*, no. 44, July 2014, p. 4.

46 *Ibid.*

47 Dmitri Alperovitch, 'Revealed: Operation Shady RAT', McAfee, August 2011.

48 Gina Chon and Charles Clover, 'US Spooks Scour China's 5-Year Plan for Hacking Clues', *Financial Times*, 25 November 2015.

49 Scott J. Henderson, 'The Dark Visitor: Inside the World of Chinese Hackers' (Lulu, 2007).

50 Nathan Thornburgh, 'Inside the Chinese Hack Attack', *Time*, 25 August 2005.

51 Sophie Borland, 'MI5 Warns Firms over China's Internet "Spying"', *Daily Telegraph*, 12 April 2008.

52 'Tracking GhostNet: Investigating a Cyber Espionage Network', Information Warfare Monitor, 29 March 2009.

53 John Leyden, '"Chinese Cyberspies" Target Energy Giants', *Register*, 10 February 2011.

54 Mathew J. Schwartz, 'Google Aurora Hack Was Chinese Counterespionage Operation', *Information Week*, 21 May 2013.

55 Alperovitch, 'Revealed'.

56 Colin Clark, 'China Attacked Internet Security Company RSA, Cyber Commander Tells SASC', *Breaking Defense*, 27 March 2012.

57 Simon Elegant, 'Enemies at the Firewall', *Time*, 6 December 2007.

58 Rose Tang, 'China–U.S. Cyber War Escalates', CNN, 1 May 2001.

59 Mandiant, 'APT1: Exposing One of China's Cyber Espionage Units', February 2013.

60 Ellen Nakashima, 'Confidential Report Lists U.S. Weapons System Designs Compromised by Chinese Cyberspies', *Washington Post*, 27 May 2013.

61 Michael S. Schmidt and David E. Sanger, '5 in China Army Face U.S. Charges of Cyberattacks', *New York Times*, 19 May 2014.

62 Novetta, 'Cyber Security Coalition Releases Full Report on Large-Scale Interdiction of Chinese State Sponsored Espionage Effort', 24 October 2014.

63 Steve Ragan, 'OPM Says Second Breach Compromised 21 Million Records', CSO, 9 July 2015.

64 Man Qi, Yongquan Wang and Rongsheng Xu, 'Fighting Cybercrime: Legislation in China', *International Journal of Electronic Security and Digital Forensics*, vol. 2, no. 2, 2009.

65 Jen Weedon, 'Testimony before the US–China Economic and Security Review Commission: Hearing on Commercial Cyber Espionage and

Barriers to Digital Trade in China', US–China Economic and Security Review Commission, 15 June 2015, http://www.uscc.gov/sites/default/files/Weedon%20Testimony.pdf.

66 Bryan Krekel, George Bakos and Christopher Barnett, 'Capability of the People's Republic of China to Conduct Cyber Warfare and Computer Network Exploitation', Northrop Grumman, in *Cyberwar Resources Guide*, no. 130, 9 October 2009.

67 'Zhongguo jundui cong wei zhichi heike huodong', *People's Daily*, 21 February 2013, http://paper.people.com.cn/rmrb/html/2013-02/21/nw.D110000renmrb_20130221_1-04.htm?div=-1.

68 Inkster, 'The Chinese Intelligence Agencies', p. 44.

69 'Obama and Xi End "Constructive" Summit', BBC, 9 June 2013.

70 'US–China Cyber Security Working Group Meets', BBC, 9 July 2013.

71 'China, US Discuss Cyber Security', Xinhua, 10 July 2013.

72 Michael D. Swaine, 'Chinese Views on Cybersecurity in Foreign Relations', *China Leadership Monitor*, no. 42, 20 September 2013.

73 US Trade Representative, '2013 Report to Congress on China's WTO Compliance', December 2013, https://ustr.gov/sites/default/files/2013-Report-to-Congress-China-WTO-Compliance.pdf.

74 David P. Fidler, 'Why the WTO Is Not an Appropriate Venue for Addressing Economic Cyber Espionage', *Arms Control Law*, 11 February 2013.

75 Zachary Goldman and Jerome A. Cohen, 'Differing Outlooks Impede Sino–US Cooperation to Enhance Cybersecurity', *South China Morning Post*, 3 August 2015.

76 'International S&T Cooperation and the Sharing of Intellectual Property', *Keji Ribao*, 13 May 1996.

77 Chen Weihuain, 'China, US Gradually Move to Manage Cyber Dispute', *China Daily*, 14 September 2015.

78 Hannah Kuchler, 'China Still Hacking U.S. Companies, Cyber Group Warns', *Financial Times*, 19 October 2015.

79 White House, 'Fact Sheet: President Xi Jinping's State Visit to the United States', 25 September 2015.

80 'First China–US Cyber Security Ministerial Dialogue Yields Positive Outcomes', Xinhua, 2 December 2015.

81 Ellen Nakashima, 'Following U.S. Indictments, China Shifts Commercial Hacking Away from Military to Civilian Agencies', *Washington Post*, 30 November 2015.

82 Peter Mattis, 'Three Scenarios for Understanding Changing PLA Activity in Cyberspace', *China Brief*, vol. 15, no. 23, 7 December 2015.

83 'Chinese Police Arrest 15,000 for Internet Crimes', Reuters, 18 August 2015.

84 Private communication, November 2015.

85 Jonathan Keane, 'DDOS Attack Hits Github After Chinese Police Force Developer to Remove Code', Digital Trends, 26 August 2015.

CHAPTER THREE

Military Cyber Capabilities

If there is one aspect of China's rise that has created widespread apprehension, it is the country's evolution into a significant military power. The development of China's armed forces since the early 1990s has been dramatic. Once reliant on a low-tech, mass-mobilisation land army designed primarily for a People's War, China has begun to attain major naval, air, space and nuclear capabilities, and is rapidly acquiring the capacity to project force beyond its borders and traditional sphere of influence. The cyber domain has been a critical factor in this evolution and, as is true for other facets of China's development, is widely regarded as a determinant of how the country will fight future wars. Understanding the precise role that cyber capabilities will play is by no means easy. As Anthony Cordesman has observed, 'China does not make publicly available a unified, single doctrine for guiding military operations.'[1] However, there is a hierarchy of official documentation that provides insight into Chinese military thinking, starting with a series of biennial defence White Papers that, although they lack specificity, give an indication of overall aims and direction. These are supplemented by articles in the journals of military think tanks such as the Academy of Military Science, official newspapers such as the *Liberation Army Daily* and the writings of serving and retired military officers.

Chinese military traditions

In assessing the cyber capabilities of the People's Liberation Army (PLA), it is important to consider China's view of the place of warfare in statecraft, and how that view might determine the ways in which these new-found capabilities will be used. Foreign analysts of China's military strategy are often preoccupied with the issue of whether it is broadly analogous to that of the country's main comparator, the United States, or qualitatively different due to the influence of traditional Chinese military thinking – requiring a different kind of analysis from those who seek to counter it. There are dangers associated with both approaches. Mirror-imaging by policymakers – assuming that an adversary will invariably interpret events and make decisions in a similar manner to oneself, or what used to be referred to in the British Foreign and Commonwealth Office as the 'Wykehamist fallacy' – has a long track record of failure, as Percy Cradock illustrates in his history of the UK Joint Intelligence Committee, *Know Your Enemy*.[2] Equally, an Orientalist view of Chinese military strategists as philosophising Go masters steeped in the traditions of Sunzi and other classical Chinese writers on strategy is likely to be just as misleading. At the same time, it is hard to imagine that an intellectual and cultural tradition developed over more than 2,000 years has not left some mark, and it is therefore worth briefly examining what that tradition actually amounts to.

At the heart of the Chinese intellectual traditions of statecraft lies a paradox equating almost to cognitive dissonance. Strongly rooted in Confucian and Daoist concepts of morality, these traditions have sought to portray China as an essentially pacifist state that privileges the civil (文) over the military (武). They emphasise a concept of defensive warfare, relying on walls and other such measures, as the natural response of an agrarian state to the kind of mobile, nomadic warfare that for most of China's history constituted the main national-security threat. In the words of Andrew Scobell, 'most Chinese strategic thinkers believe that Chinese strategic culture is pacifist, defensive-minded, and nonexpansionist.'[3] This perception is further strengthened by the well-established concept of *yi zhan* (Just War), the basis of which is set out in some detail in the texts that emerged during the era of Warring States (circa 475–221 BCE) – and which include justifications for invading another country to overthrow an oppressive ruler, a practice that is anathema to the modern Chinese state. Another important influence on perceptions both in China and overseas has been a focus on the best-known classical treatise on strategy and warfare, Sunzi's *Sunzi Bingfa* (Art of War), particularly that work's emphasis on *bu zhan er dai* (achieving victory without engaging in hostilities).

Such cognitive dissonance is hardly unique to China: most countries have a benign view of themselves and their strategic intentions, and few, if any, have chosen to engage in warfare without believing right to be on their side. But, until relatively recently, most Western countries saw offensive warfare as an essential adjunct to statecraft, and did not seek to pretend otherwise. In China's case, however, the Confucian pacifist narrative stands in stark contrast to a reality in which the country's offensive warfare and expansionism has been a constant feature of its history, right up until the present day. In his book *Cultural Realism*, US scholar Alastair Iain Johnston analyses this dichotomy through a study of *Sunzi Bingfa* and six other classics of Chinese strategy,[4] combined with an assessment of the strategies adopted by rulers of the Ming dynasty (1368–1644) in their struggle against the Mongols. Johnston posits what he terms a 'parabellum strategic culture', characterised by hard-headed realpolitik in which the use of military force is seen as a first resort, the aim of which is to achieve a comprehensive victory.[5] Pacifist policies are regarded as preparing the way for offensive military operations or buying time to remedy vulnerabilities. Johnston points out that the Ming dynasty mounted more than one offensive military operation in each year of its existence. Neither was the Qing dynasty (1644–1911) above exporting violence, even engaging in an episode of gunboat diplomacy with Mexico in the 1870s. And, since the 1949 founding of the People's Republic, China has launched offensive military operations on the Korean Peninsula, Quemoy and Matsu islands, and the Ussuri river – as well as in Vietnam, in the Orwellian-sounding 'Counterattack in Self-Defence' (the latter, though strategically successful, highlighted many operational shortcomings of a PLA that had not fought a major conflict since the Korean War).

The current rhetoric of the Chinese state continues the tradition of emphasising China's peaceful intentions while acquiring ever greater military resources. Since 1998, successive iterations of Chinese defence White Papers have delivered variations of the message in the preface of the 2015 edition:

> China will unswervingly follow the path of peaceful development, pursue an independent foreign policy of peace and a national defense policy that is defensive in nature, oppose hegemonism and power politics in all forms, and will never seek hegemony or expansion. China's armed forces will remain a staunch force in maintaining world peace.

The document defines the country's concept of *zhudong fangyu* (Active Defence) as 'adherence to the unity of strategic defense and operational and tactical offense; adherence to the principles of defense, self-defense and post-emptive [sic] strike; and adherence to the stance that "we will not attack unless we are attacked, but we will surely counterattack if attacked"'.[6]

This declaratory policy is reinforced by China's well-established position of 'no first use' of nuclear weapons, and by its insistence that the cyber domain should not become militarised. However, some aspects of China's approach to national defence have raised concerns among Western governments and analysts about the strategy's true purpose and direction. One such concern relates to the perception that China lacks transparency in its acquisition of defence capabilities, a criticism frequently voiced by senior US policymakers.[7] Beijing rejects this argument, but PLA officers have said at conferences that China is reluctant to put all its military cards on the table due to its negative experiences with Western powers in the nineteenth and twentieth centuries. Another widely held concern is that China is under-reporting its defence expenditure by, inter alia, failing to factor in various types of scientific and technical research[8] – again, an assertion that Beijing rebuts.

Yet another concern is linked with evidence of what seems to be a carefully nurtured culture of anti-Western paranoia within China's military. A prime example of this mindset can be found in the 2013 film *Jiaoliang Wusheng* (*Silent Contest*), produced by the Information Management Centre of the National Defense University.[9] Slightly more than two hours long, the film features interviews with three serving PLA generals and – to the strains of the theme music from *Game of Thrones* – reflects the view that the West, particularly the US, has always been hostile towards China, and has sought to undermine both the country and the Chinese Communist Party (CCP) through a concerted programme of subversion and the promotion of Western values and institutions. It depicts the world in starkly Manichaean terms, and warns of the struggle to come. Similar views have become ever more prevalent in PLA newspapers and journals since President Xi Jinping came to power.[10] Some allowance needs to be made for the fact that such material is designed to inculcate and reinforce loyalty to the Party, and to promote a greater sense of public duty and aversion to corruption. Nonetheless, the approach is likely to have a profound effect over time, especially given that most of those at whom it is directed will have little, if any, experience of life outside China or access to alternative narratives. These considerations, combined with the speed at which the PLA is modernising and the growing scope of China's global ambitions, have led one Western scholar to conclude that the country has for decades pursued a strategy of lulling Western nations into a false sense of security about its intentions, while quietly building the capabilities needed to displace the US as the global hegemon.[11]

The PLA: An army for the Party, not the nation

An important factor in analysing China's approach to military matters is the reality that the PLA is explicitly not a national army but rather the army of the CCP. The key oversight mechanism for the PLA is the Party's Central Military Commission (CMC), whose chairman is Xi, in his capacity as CCP secretary-general. The importance of this position can be illustrated by the fact that, when the leadership of the Party passed from Jiang Zemin to Hu Jintao in 2003, Jiang held on to the chairmanship of the CMC for a further two years, substantially constraining Hu's grasp on power. Xi, by contrast, assumed all of his current positions simultaneously. There is no state body that has the capacity to oversee, or exercise policy influence over, the PLA: the Ministry of National Defense has thus far served only to provide China with an institutional docking point for engagement with other states on military matters (although its status and significance may be about to increase).

The primacy of the PLA's political role long predates the founding of the People's Republic. In the course of the Gutian Conference, convened on 1 November 1929 in the village of that name in Fujian Province, Mao Zedong insisted on the subordination to the Party of the PLA's predecessor, the Fourth Army of the Chinese Workers' and Peasants' Red Army. In his capacity as the Comintern-appointed political commissar, Mao criticised what he referred to as 'the purely military viewpoint', embodied in the proposition that military affairs took precedence over politics and that the role of the Red Army was simply to fight.[12] Mao insisted that the Red Army should carry out the political tasks of the revolution, and should engage in propaganda work among the masses. This view was to be reflected many years later in Hu's 2004 New Historic Missions of the Armed Forces in the New Period of the New Century, which, in addition to emphasising the PLA's political allegiance to the Party, expanded its remit to supporting national economic development.[13] The Gutian Conference was, as argued by James Mulvenon, 'the seminal moment where the principle of CCP control of the military was enshrined as core party doctrine, and "set the tone for the army's political work during the revolutionary era and beyond"'.[14]

Marking the 85th anniversary of the conference, Xi convened in Gutian a meeting of around 420 senior military leaders, including all serving members of the CMC. The event was preceded by an article written by Yu Guang and published in the July 2014 issue of the Party theoretical journal Qiushi, which sought to emphasise the continuing importance of the CCP's leadership of the military, and the role of people as the determinants of the outcome of wars. Reflecting PLA propaganda, Guang described a backcloth of external threats from Western forces. They, he argued, aimed to promote universal values and constitutional democracy by 'pointing the spears of Westernisation at the Chinese military in a reckless attempt to pull the Chinese military from under the Party's banner', by championing ideas such as the conversion of the PLA into a state institution. Xi used the conference to reinforce the central-ity of Party control and the importance of improving political work, particularly that to combat corruption.[15]

The issues of corruption and Party control of the PLA had become increasingly vexed during the tenure of Hu, who was unable to exert firm control over a military leadership that was entrenched, unaccountable and corrupt. Between 2002 and 2012, generals Xu Caihou and Guo Boxiong controlled the mili-tary's senior-appointments system through a system of bribery so pervasive that almost all the PLA officers who attended Xi's meeting in Gutian would have paid for their promotions. According to serving PLA major-generals, the going rate for an appointment as commander of one of China's seven mili-tary regions was 20 million RMB (US$3.25m).[16] The CCP's public censure of Xu and Guo, in 2014 and 2015 respectively, can be seen as on a par with the arrest of security chief Zhou Yongkang, as part of a concerted effort to remove vested inter-ests and reassert Party control – moves the leadership saw as prerequisites for reform. The CCP still regards this effort as a work in progress, as evidenced by the announcement of a reor-ganisation of the PLA command structure in articles published by state media outlets in November 2015. In the making for a decade, the reform involves a shift from the old structure of seven military regions to what was initially intended to be five such regions – North, South, East, West and Central – and the restructuring of the CMC into 15 departments, incorporat-ing some located in the PLA General Staff and the Ministry of

National Defense.[17] A significant driver of the undertaking has been the perceived need to move away from reliance on land forces and towards a system based on joint service structures, a design more appropriate to the modern era and more in line with other militaries, particularly that of the US. The *Liberation Daily News* published in December 2015 a commentary stating that the status quo challenged the CCP's absolute leadership of the military, and that the purpose of the reform was to consolidate the CMC's power.[18]

The very public struggle for effective political control of the PLA may cast light on its influence over China's foreign and security policies. Analysts have puzzled over the extent to which some recent military actions – including a 2007 test in which the PLA destroyed a low-earth-orbit satellite with a ballistic missile,[19] and the flight of China's J-20 stealth fighter in January 2011, during a visit to China by then US secretary of defense Robert Gates[20] – were properly coordinated at the policy level. In neither case did China's state institutions appear to have advance notice of the events in question. And, in respect of the earlier test, it is hard to imagine China's leadership having approved an action that generated an unprecedented quantity of low-earth-orbit space debris, causing significant damage to China's international reputation. The PLA has for some time had no representation in the Politburo Standing Committee, China's top policy body, and only two representatives in the wider Politburo. Thus, in formal terms, the military has arguably less scope for direct influence over policy than at any time since the People's Republic was established. In practice, however, the PLA has been given a high degree of operational latitude by the leadership, and is hence able to shape the policy debate through its actions on the ground. It is not fanciful to imagine that one of Xi's objectives in asserting greater political control of the PLA was to improve China's risk management, at a time when the country appears to be testing its boundaries in the international-security arena.

Evidence of corruption at the heart of the PLA's leadership and questions about where its loyalty really lies have fostered doubts about its effectiveness as a fighting force.[21] Some have even questioned whether the PLA is actually built for conflict or is intended to serve the purpose of deterrence. But, while it faces enormous challenges in evolving to the point where it is on a par with the US military, the PLA has developed a formidable array of weaponry and has exercised intensively to acquire the skills needed for conflict in the twenty-first century. And there is much less evidence of corruption in the PLA's front-line units than at headquarters level: it is, after all, in areas such as logistics and personnel where the opportunities for corruption are mostly to be found. Furthermore, it is simply inconceivable that any of China's potential adversaries might plan on the presumption that, on the day, the PLA might not fight. Even if initially things went badly for PLA forces, which given their lack of combat experience may well be the case, national prestige would require a doubling down of effort. While continuing to analyse the shortcomings in China's military performance, potential adversaries might do well to recall the view of Second World War US general Joseph 'Vinegar Joe' Stilwell that properly led Chinese troops could be the equal of any he had commanded.[22]

From People's War to RMA with Chinese characteristics

Until the 1980s, the prevailing PLA military doctrine was the Maoist concept of People's War, an essentially defensive strategy that involved luring an invading force into the Chinese heartland, where it would eventually be isolated and overwhelmed. During Mao's rule, however, China engaged in a succession of offensive attacks (as detailed above) that were justified through his expansion of the concept of *zhengyi zhanzheng* (Just War) to sanction warfare that was either defensive in nature or designed to preserve national unity (Quemoy, Matsu), combat hegemonism or promote class struggle (Korea, Ussuri river, Vietnam). People's War was a quintessentially low-tech phenomenon reflecting Mao's assertion *jueding zhanzheng shengfude shi ren er bushi wu* (people, not objects, determine victory or defeat in warfare).[23] Although Chinese military thinking has undergone considerable evolution since the Mao era, the PLA sees the concept of People's War as having continued validity. The concept is set out in the 2001 edition of *The Science of Military Strategy*, a periodic publication of the Academy of Military Science:

> The cooperation between regular warfare and irregular warfare stresses that we should give full play to the creativity of the masses and servicemen on the basis of inheriting the glorious tradition of the people's war so that the new form of people's war under modern conditions can be explored according to the reality of the war in different strategic directions.[24]

China's use of cyber militias arguably continues the People's War tradition.

In the mid-1980s, Deng Xiaoping, China's de facto leader, introduced the concept of Active Defence into Chinese military thinking. Active Defence was conceived of as an exercise in *ju diren yu guomen zhi wai* (resisting the enemy outside the gates of the nation), with the emphasis on bringing any conflict to a speedy conclusion. The 2001 edition of *The Science of Military Strategy* lists the three pillars of the concept as: China will not fire the first shot and will attempt to settle any dispute by peaceful means for as long as possible; China will attempt to deter war militarily or politically before it breaks out; and China will respond to an attack with offensive action and will seek to destroy the enemy's forces, and it will not be the first to use or threaten to use nuclear weapons.[25]

Under Active Defence, a Chinese military response can be sparked by not only kinetic action but also political or other strategic moves[26] – an issue that is becoming increasingly relevant to the cyber domain. Since 1993, Active Defence has been operationalised through a concept of operations variously referred to as *gaojishu tiaojianxia de jubu zhanzheng* (fighting local wars under hi-tech conditions) and *xinxihua tiaojianxia de jubu zhanzheng* (fighting local wars under conditions of informatisation). The former term emerged during the tenure of Jiang and the latter under Hu, reflecting the evolution in technology that had taken place, but the two are to all intents and purposes interchangeable. The concept envisages the PLA as being involved primarily in wars around China's periphery that are limited in scope and duration, bringing conflicts to a swift, decisive end by relying on information and communications technologies (ICTs) to acquire an operational advantage over an adversary.

For China's military and political leaders, the apparent ease with which the US and its allies defeated a largely Soviet-equipped Iraqi army during the First Gulf War created a moment of epiphany.[27] The event amplified an emerging interest in the Western concept of the Revolution in Military Affairs (RMA), initially viewed with suspicion by many in the PLA, who cleaved to Mao's doctrine of 'people, not objects'. In the aftermath of the conflict, a time when it was still struggling with the challenge of mechanisation, the PLA began a serious, sustained effort to develop informationised capabilities. The 1990s saw the publication of a significant body of writing by Chinese strategists such as Wang Baocun, Wang Pufeng, Wei

Jincheng and Shen Weiguang, much of whose work was translated and collected in the 1997 publication *Chinese Views of Future Warfare*, edited by Michael Pillsbury.[28] Wang Baocun, a scholar at the Academy of Military Science, talked of information warfare as presenting China with a unique opportunity to catch up with the West. Wang Pufeng, often referred to as the 'father of Chinese IW [information warfare]', emphasised the importance of achieving *zhixinxiquan* (information dominance) in the early stages of conflict, and spoke of IW's potential to produce 'soft casualties' by damaging the information capabilities of an adversary and creating military outcomes with minimal loss of life. At the same time, he observed that China had a long way to go: 'the authorized strength and equipment, strategy, tactics and military theory of China's military are still basically the products of the industrial era and are far from satisfying the demands of information warfare'.[29]

The early Chinese exponents of IW saw the practice as very much an asymmetric response to a stronger opponent. This perception was most famously articulated in the 1999 book *Unrestricted Warfare*, written by PLA Air Force colonels Qiao Liang and Wang Xiangsui. The central thesis of this work is that, in the modern era, warfare cannot be restricted to the battlefield and needs to be fought on all fronts. The book seizes on the US military's dependence on ICTs for war fighting, and argues for pre-emptive cyber operations to degrade its ability to fight. In the words of the authors, 'technological progress has given us the means to strike at the enemy's nerve centre directly without harming other things, giving us numerous new options for achieving victory, and all these make people believe that the best way to achieve victory is to control, not to kill.'[30]

The other concept that gained much traction among China's strategic thinkers in that period was the so-called *shashoujian*

(assassin's mace), a term that has given rise to much specu-
lation and discussion. (A weapon used in traditional Chinese
martial arts, the *shashoujian* is light, easily concealable and has
several angled edges; it is designed to deliver a blow that will
penetrate armour and comprehensively disable an opponent.)
The term seems to have originated from a group of PLA thinkers linked to the pro-RMA school, who advocated asymmetric,
China-specific methods for modernising IW. As argued by one
such thinker, Major-General Xu Yanbin, 'we should combine
Western technology with Eastern wisdom. This is our trump
card for winning a 21st century war.'[31] The concept was taken
up in 1999 by Jiang, who, at a meeting of the CMC, emphasised
the need to develop a suite of *shashoujian* weapons in the aftermath of NATO bombing in Kosovo. The upshot of this was the
establishment of State Security Project 998, which was aimed at
accelerating 'the research, development and installation of new
weapons ... to resist US hegemonism'.[32]

The perceived need to develop *shashoujian* became more
pressing in 2000, when the US declared that it regarded China as
a strategic competitor, and Taiwan's government, led by Chen
Shui-bian, seemed bent on reversing the gradual trend towards
reunification. That year, Beijing announced the establishment
of the 112 Project and the 126 Programme, both designed to
develop new advanced weaponry. No weapon developed
within China has ever been publicly categorised as part of a
shashoujian programme – and, indeed, the use of the term is
seen as sensitive in Chinese policy circles. But if a *shashoujian* is
viewed as being concealed until the point of use, sudden and
unexpected in its deployment, and devastating in its effects, it
is possible to identify various items in the PLA inventory that
might fit within such a programme: precision-guided muni-
tions, advanced submarines, nuclear weapons and, of course,
IW capabilities.

China's IW concepts and doctrines

In 2002 Jiang told the 16th Party Congress that 'our national defence and army building should keep in line with the world's military transformation' – a statement that effectively endorsed the RMA approach.[33] China's 2004 defence White Paper announced an RMA with Chinese characteristics, which had IW at its core:

> To take the road of composite and leapfrog development. Going with the tide of the world's military development and moving along the direction of informationalization in the process of modernization, the People's Liberation Army (PLA) shall gradually achieve the transition from mechanization and semi-mechanization to informationalization.[34]

Since then, the PLA has sought to integrate IW into its military doctrine and practice, in an apparent bid to draw closer to acquiring the perceived capabilities of the US. Ironically, this requires the PLA to increase its network dependency, and hence to forfeit some of the asymmetric advantages identified in *Unrestricted Warfare*. The mainstreaming of IW took place at the same time that joint operations – later termed 'integrated joint operations' – were being progressively introduced. The PLA also adopted the Western training concept of 'blue' and 'red' forces, replacing an exercise model of large-scale set-piece manoeuvres with one that required a non-linear approach centred on improvisation and adaptation. As a consequence, the PLA now has at least 12 informationised training facilities, allowing its field units to undertake exercises that feature realistic combined-arms training in which jamming and interference degrade their communications.[35] The military's 2007 manual *Outline for Military Training and Evaluation* specifies that all service arms

should place exercises in complex electromagnetic environ-
ments at the core of campaign and tactical training. Major PLA
exercises conducted since 2008 – such as *Kuayue 2009*, *Shiming
Xingdong 2010* and *Lianhe 2011* – have had important defensive
and offensive cyber- and information-operations components.
Meanwhile, military departments for information, strategic
planning and training were either established or repurposed to
promote informatisation. In 2010 the PLA set up the Information
Safeguards Base, with the aim of addressing cyber threats and
protecting information security and infrastructure.[36]

A key driver for these developments has been Washington's
decision to establish a Cyber Command, and with it a declaratory policy that reserves the right to respond to cyber attacks
in whatever way it sees fit. Chinese diplomats, policymakers
and academics regularly criticise the move as encouraging the
militarisation of cyberspace and pursuing the absolute security of the US at the expense of other states. Beijing's official
position is that China possesses no offensive cyber capabilities,
and that those developed by the PLA are purely defensive.
However, the reality of Chinese IW positions offence and
pre-emption as critical to success. China's military doctrine
defines information supremacy as essential to achieving battlefield supremacy. Information supremacy can only be gained
through pre-emptive offensive operations because, if the PLA
waits for an adversary to strike first, it risks having its networks
disabled and hence finding itself without the capacity to retali-
ate.[37] Viewed in more positive terms, an effective information
campaign can potentially achieve a decisive outcome at low
cost and with minimal casualties. Such operations are relevant
to the PLA's anti-access/area-denial strategy in the Taiwan
Strait and the South and East China seas, which is designed to
prevent the entry of US forces into these waters long enough
for China to achieve its strategic objectives.[38]

Chinese military strategy combines IW and electronic warfare into the single concept of *wangdian yitizhan* (Integrated Network Electronic Warfare), a termed coined by General Dai Qingmin, former commander of the Fourth Department of the PLA General Staff (4/PLA). The PLA has also developed the concept of *xinxi duikang* (Information Confrontation), which seeks to combine all elements of IW, electronic and otherwise, under a single command authority. The non-electronic elements of IW include psychological operations and deception. The underlying concept is referred to as a *tixi zuo zhan* (system of systems) operation. As detailed in a 2012 report prepared by Northrop Grumman for the US–China Economic and Security Review Commission, this involves

> using information systems and networks to create a common integrated command infrastructure that links multiple complex 'macro-systems' associated with different weapons platforms, C4ISR systems, and units regardless of the domain in which they operate. Information warfare, in the context of systems operation theory, is viewed by some PLA authors as one of many combat macro-systems to be integrated under this concept, but one with the ability to influence battlefield perception, information transmission and command networks. The systems operations concept fundamentally emphasizes linking all service branches into a common operating picture that can be accessed at multiple echelons of command.[39]

A potentially significant development in this concept came in January 2016, when China announced the establishment of three new military units: the PLA General Command, the PLA Rocket Force and the intriguingly named PLA Strategic

Support Force. The PLA Rocket Force appears to be a revamped version of the Second Artillery Force, reclassified as a full service arm to reflect the fact that it now oversees not only an arsenal of strategic nuclear-armed missiles but also an array of conventional precision-guided missiles with various ranges. The Strategic Support Force was rather unhelpfully described by a Ministry of National Defense spokesman as combining 'the strategic, basic and support resources of the country's new type of combat forces'[40] – and slightly more helpfully by Chinese military expert Song Zhongping as 'aimed at providing resources capable of protecting China's cyber and space security'.[41] Although it is logical to group oversight of cyber and space operations in one organisation given the close relationship between the domains, the move was arguably a setback for the PLA Air Force, which might have aspired to mirror its US counterpart in assuming responsibility for space. The creation of the Strategic Support Force appears to involve the integration of the *zongcan sanbu* and the *zongcan sibu* (Third and Fourth departments of the PLA General Staff, or 3/PLA and 4/PLA respectively) – the former responsible for signals intelligence (SIGINT), and the latter for radar operations and electronic countermeasures – with elements of the PLA General Political Department, which oversees information operations, propaganda and psychological warfare. Overall, the changes highlight the importance that the PLA attaches to an integrated approach to cyber, electronic and space warfare.

While the PLA's long-term objectives are clear enough, there is no easy way to gauge its progress towards achieving them. Most militaries are struggling to integrate cyber operations and IW into their operational capabilities, and all suffer from the same problems: a lack of information-technology skills, and the gap between a young generation familiar with ICTs and an older generation of less technically literate officers. The

PLA also has to complete the process of mechanisation while simultaneously promoting informatisation, and to contend with the reality that US forces are far more advanced in terms of their reach and capabilities within the cyber domain. China regularly accuses the US of engaging in a pre-emptive (by implication, against China) IW campaign that 'could cause unforeseeable disastrous consequences for human society',[42] and a key Chinese strategic objective is to diminish US preponderance in the cyber domain through a variety of approaches, most of them diplomatic (see Chapter Four). Like the militaries of several other states, the PLA has sought to route as many of its communications as possible through fibre-optic land lines. And it has developed the BeiDou satellite-positioning system to reduce its dependence on the US Global Positioning System. Furthermore, much Chinese research has focused on developing capabilities to destroy or degrade the satellites on which the US military is perceived to be uniquely dependent.[43] Such work has obvious escalatory implications, but so far there is no indication that the PLA has developed any clear doctrine or processes for managing such escalation, or a model for de-escalation – despite the efforts of Western scholars to raise the issue with Chinese officers.

A key element of PLA thinking on the cyber domain is that of *weishe* (deterrence). Deterrence is normally thought of in the West as using the threat of force to discourage an adversary from undertaking a hostile action, and as taking one of three forms. These forms are denial, or preventing an adversary from making gains through a particular action; punishment, or persuading an adversary that the punitive consequences of an action will outweigh its benefits; and entanglement, or convincing an adversary that its interests are so intertwined with those of the state it is planning to attack that any aggression will damage it just as much as it will the target of aggression. By contrast, the Chinese concept of *weishe* is, in the words of one Western scholar, 'more expansive and normative than the US use, encompassing threat or menace'.[44] In the words of another, '*weishe* includes the Western concepts of deterrence and compellence'.[45] Chinese military writings on *weishe* highlight what is seen as a more principled approach to deterrence than that of the Western model, arguing for the concept as a means to defend legitimate interests without resorting to actual hostilities – again, a reflection of Sunzi's *bu zhan er dai*. However, Chinese military thinkers also recognise the difficulties of pursuing this objective in a domain as inherently ambiguous as cyberspace, where it can be challenging to identify and attribute actions, and to predict the impact of any response. The US has experienced a range of cyber attacks that it has attributed to China, including intrusions into critical infrastructure such as the power grid.[46] But it is impossible to determine whether such activities are reconnaissance, an attempt at signalling or both. And it is often unclear whether such activity was undertaken by a state entity or with state approval.

Another unknown is whether Chinese strategic thinkers see cyber deterrence as a practice that should be restricted to the cyber domain or one that can involve the kind of cross-domain retaliation that the US has reserved a right to – and has arguably exercised, given Washington's use of legal action to respond to Chinese state-sponsored commercial espionage. China regards cross-domain deterrence as posing considerable difficulties, and is therefore less than anxious to address it in international negotiations. Chinese scholars, diplomats and military officers point to the lack of international consensus on what constitutes a cyber attack or a cyber weapon; how issues of proportionality and discrimination should be addressed in a domain used for both civilian and military purposes; the extent of a state's responsibility for actions undertaken on its networks; and how to deal with the issue of a state's neutrality when attacks are routed through the networks of other countries. That said, the overall thrust of Chinese thinking on IW suggests that, in a time of war, the PLA would not hesitate to attack elements of civilian infrastructure – including finance and banking, transport and other public utilities – with the aim of eroding the will to resist of those living in the adversary state.

Military cyber units

In developing cyber-warfare and IW capabilities, most militaries look to their national SIGINT agencies to provide the required systems and skills. In many countries, SIGINT has traditionally been the preserve of the military, and even civilian SIGINT agencies, such as those of the US and the United Kingdom, have strong connections with and provide operational support for their armed forces. Another common characteristic of SIGINT agencies in the Information Age is their development of relationships with universities and private companies to acquire the research and operational skills that they cannot generate in-house. In these particulars, China is little different from any other state. While 3/PLA is heavily involved in cyber-espionage operations (see Chapter Two), it also appears to have primary responsibility for computer-network defence. In contrast, 4/PLA has primary responsibility for computer-network attacks: operations to denigrate or destroy enemy networks. However, there is a third military actor which may have responsibilities similar to those of 3/PLA and 4/PLA: the Second Artillery Force. The latter is tasked with directly targeting enemy centres of gravity, and it is believed to have devoted considerable effort to analysing the impact of single points of failure within the infrastructure of major adversaries.[47]

An important focus of Chinese military cyber capabilities has been leveraging the skills and capabilities to be found within the civilian sector. The State Council's Medium- and Long-term Program for Science and Technology Development 2006–2020 emphasises the importance of integrating civilian and military scientific and technical efforts.[48] And China's 11th Five-Year Plan discusses the prospect of *junmin ronghua* (merging the military with the civilian).[49] In the cyber domain, the PLA is developing links with universities and the civilian telecommunications sector. The military's interactions with Chinese telecommunications companies range from the occasional and ad hoc through to the close and collaborative – with entities such as ZTE and Huawei having significant ties to the PLA.[50] The military also has collaborative research relationships with around 46 universities.

Cyber militias, which likely have a collective membership of more than 10m people, are another important force multiplier for 3/PLA. Such entities have been in existence since the turn of the millennium, and the Academy of Military Science endorsed them as a concept in 2006. These militias are sometimes situated within civilian corporations – of which China Mobile is an egregious example – and within universities. The exact role and functions of these units is unknown but, as a general principle, the main role of militias is, in the words of Dennis Blasko, 'providing rear area security … for PLA active duty units as well as the civilian population; logistics support; and repair of infrastructure damaged from long-range strikes on China … [The] majority of them do not add to the PLA's power projection capabilities.'[51] It is probable that China's cyber militias also function in this way. Indeed, it is hard to see how the PLA could allow them to have an offensive function, since any attacks they undertake could undermine or negate more advanced operations conducted by regular military units.

In summary, it is unlikely that the detail of China's military cyber strategies and capabilities will come to light anytime soon, not least because the country seems to increasingly see uncertainty as a key element of its strategic armoury. So, we will be left to try and interpret often weak signals as best we can. When it comes to the cyber domain, the PLA sees informatisation as essential to its overall military-modernisation programme – and it has made strenuous efforts to push forward this process, with IW now firmly integrated into all major PLA military exercises. But it remains the case that, as it struggles to situate the role of cyber warfare within its overall strategic framework (like all militaries), the PLA lacks many of the capabilities needed to realise its ambitious plans, and continues to have a strong sense of vulnerability vis-à-vis the US. It is unclear whether China has realistic expectations of what can be achieved through cyber warfare – in this context, one is reminded of the expectations of airpower, which proved overly optimistic – and whether the country's more hubristic utterances are intended as a form of deterrence. But what we can infer is that China will use its growing cyber power to seek to intimidate and coerce weaker opponents, asserting all the while that its cause is just. And, in the event of conflict with the US or another powerful country, China's use of cyber capabilities will not be limited to achieving tactical battlefield effects, but will be deployed at the outset to disable the adversary – with all the escalatory risk that would entail. Until such a moment arrives, a key focus of China's strategy will be to shape an international environment that erodes the strategic primacy of potential adversaries, particularly the significant first-mover advantage enjoyed by the US and its allies. In this context, Beijing sees international negotiations on cyber governance and cyber security as playing a vital role in shaping the battlespace within which the PLA may need to manoeuvre.

Notes

1   Anthony Cordesman, *Chinese Strategic Military Power 2014: Chinese, Japanese, Korean, Taiwanese and US Perspectives* (Lanham, MD: Rowman & Littlefield, 2014), p. 134.

2   Percy Cradock, *Know Your Enemy: How the Joint Intelligence Committee Saw the World* (London: John Murray, 2002).

3   Andrew Scobell, 'China and Strategic Culture', Strategic Studies Institute, May 2002, p. 4.

4   The classics studied by Johnston are *Sunzi Bingfa, Wuzi Bingfa, Sima Fa, Wei Liao Zi, San Lue, Liu Tao* and *Wen Dui*.

5   Alastair Iain Johnston, *Cultural Realism: Strategic Culture and Grand Strategy in Chinese History* (Princeton, NJ: Princeton University Press, 1995).

6   State Council Information Office of the People's Republic of China, 'China's Military Strategy', May 2015, http://eng.mod.gov.cn/Database/WhitePapers/index.htm.

7   Paul Eckert, 'Pentagon Criticises China on Military Transparency', Reuters, 25 March 2009.

8   IISS, *The Military Balance 2015* (Abingdon: Routledge for the IISS, 2015), pp. 215–16.

9   The video can be accessed – in Chinese only – at https://www.youtube.com/watch?v=M_8lSjcoSW8.

10 'Jue buneng rang hulianwang cheng renxin liushidi', *Liberation Army Daily*, 12 May 2015, http://news.mod.gov.cn/headlines/2015-05/12/content_4584573.htm.

11 Michael Pillsbury, *The Hundred Year Marathon: China's Secret Strategy to Replace America as the Global Superpower* (New York: Henry Holt, 2015).

12 'Draft Resolution of the Ninth Congress of the Chinese Communist Party in the Fourth Red Army', in Stuart R. Schram and Nancy J. Hodes (eds), *Mao's Road to Power: Revolutionary Writings 1912–1949* (Armonk, NY: East Gate Publishing, 1995), p. 196.

13 James Mulvenon, 'Chairman Hu and the PLA's "New Historic Missions"', *China Leadership Monitor*, no. 27, Winter 2009, http://www.hoover.org/research/chairman-hu-and-plas-new-historic-missions.

14 James Mulvenon, 'Hotel Gutian: We Haven't Had That Spirit Here Since 1929', *China Leadership Monitor*, no. 46, http://www.hoover.org/research/hotel-gutian-we-havent-had-spirit-here-1929.

15 *Ibid.*

16 'Shaojiang baoliao: jiakong Hu Jintao Hu Caihou biaojia maiguan dajunqu siling liangqianwan', *Xingdao Ribao*, 10 March 2015, http://news.singtao.ca/toronto/2015-03-10/world1425970399d5474726.html.

17 The new departments are: the General Office, the Joint Staff Department, the Political Work Department, the Logistic Support Department, the Equipment Development Department, the Training and Administration Department, the National Defence Mobilisation Department, the Discipline Inspection Commission, the Politics and Law Commission, the Science and Technology Commission, the Office for Strategic Planning, the Office for Reform

and Organisational Structure, the Office for International Military Cooperation, the Audit Office and the Agency for Offices Administration. See: 'China's New Central Military Commission Organ Established', China Miltiary Online, 11 January 2016.

18 Minnie Chan, 'PLA Reform: China's Top Brass Set New Year Deadline for Military Command Structure', *South China Morning Post*, 8 December 2015.

19 Ashley J. Tellis, 'China's Military Space Strategy', *Survival*, vol. 49, no. 3, Autumn 2007.

20 Elisabeth Bumiller and Michael Wines, 'Test of Stealth Fighter Clouds Gates Visit to China', *New York Times*, 11 January 2011.

21 John Garnaut, 'All the Toys, but Can China Fight?', *Sydney Morning Herald*, 27 April 2013.

22 Barbara W. Tuchman, *Stilwell and the American Experience in China 1911–1945* (New York: MacMillan, 1971).

23 Nicholas A. Budak, '"Winning the Battle Without Fighting": Strategic Culture and Information Warfare in the People's Liberation Army of China', honours thesis, 2014, http://arminda.whitman.edu/theses/188/.

24 Peng Guangqian and Yao Youzhi (eds), *The Science of Military Strategy* (Beijing: Military Science Publishing House, 2001), p. 376.

25 *Ibid.*, p. 99.

26 Dennis J. Blasko, *The Chinese Army Today: Tradition and Transformation in the 21st Century* (New York: Routledge, 2012), p. 124.

27 Timothy L. Thomas, *Dragon Bytes: Chinese Information-War Theory and Practice* (Fort Leavenworth, KS: Foreign Military Studies Office, 2004), p. 5.

28 Michael Pillsbury (ed.), *Chinese Views of Future Warfare* (Washington DC: National Defense University Press, 1997).

29 Wang Pufeng, 'The Challenge of Information Warfare', *China Military Science*, Spring 1995, http://fas.org/irp/world/china/docs/iw_mg_wang.htm.

30 Qiao Liang and Wang Xiangsui, *Unrestricted Warfare* (Beijing: PLA Literature and Arts Publishing House, 1999).

31 Jason E. Bruzdzinski, 'Demystifying Sha Shou Jian: China's "Assassin's Mace" Concept', in Andrew Scobell and Larry Wortzel (eds), *Civil–Military Change in China: Elites, Institutes, and Ideas after the 16th Party Congress* (Strategic Studies Institute, September 2004), p. 319.

32 *Ibid.*, pp. 312–29.

33 *Ibid.*, p. 319.

34 State Council Information Office of the People's Republic of China, 'China's National Defense in 2004', 27 December 2004, http://fas.org/nuke/guide/china/doctrine/natdef2004.html#1.

35 Bryan Krekel, 'Capability of the People's Republic of China to Conduct Cyber Warfare and Computer Network Exploitation', Northrop Grumman, 9 October 2009, http://cryptocomb.org/NorthropGrumman_PRC_Cyber_Paper_FINAL_Approved%20Report_16Oct2009.pdf.

36 IISS, *The Military Balance 2011* (Abingdon: Routledge for the IISS, 2015), p. 29.

[37] Dai Qingmin, *Wangdian Yitizhan* (Beijing: People's Liberation Army Press, 2002), p. 153.

[38] For an analysis of this strategy and its implications, see Aaron L. Friedberg, *A Contest for Supremacy: China, America and the Struggle for Mastery in Asia* (Oxford: Routledge for the IISS, 2011).

[39] Bryan Krekel, Patton Adams and George Bakos, 'Occupying the Information High Ground: Chinese Capabilities for Computer Network Operations and Cyber Espionage', Northrop Grumman, 7 March 2012, p. 17.

[40] Wu Gang, 'China Upgrades Missile Force, Adds Space and Cyber War Forces', *Global Times*, 1 January 2016.

[41] *Ibid.*

[42] Michael D. Swaine, 'Chinese Views on Cybersecurity in Foreign Relations', *China Leadership Monitor*, no. 42, 7 October 2013, pp. 8–9, http://carnegieendowment.org/files/CLM42MS.pdf.

[43] Franz-Stefan Gady, 'Revealed: China Tests Secret Missile Capable of Hitting US Satellites', *Diplomat*, 11 November 2015.

[44] Adam Segal, 'A Chinese View on Why Cyber Deterrence is So Hard', Council on Foreign Relations, 11 January 2012.

[45] Kevin Pollpeter, 'Chinese Writings on Cyberwarfare and Coercion', in Jon R. Lindsay, Tai Ming Cheung and Derek S. Reveron (eds), *China and Cybersecurity: Espionage, Strategy, and Politics in the Digital Domain* (Oxford: Oxford University Press, 2015), p. 147.

[46] 'Cyber Spies Assault US Power Grid', *Jane's Intelligence Digest*, 5 May 2009.

[47] Mark A. Stokes, 'The Chinese People's Liberation Army Computer Network Operations Infrastructure', in Lindsay, Cheung and Reveron (eds), *China and Cybersecurity*, p. 175.

[48] Ministry of Science and Technology of the People's Republic of China, 'National Outline for Medium and Long Term Science and Technology Development Planning (2006–2020)', *China Science and Technology Newsletter*, no. 456, February 2006, http://www.most.gov.cn/eng/newsletters/2006/200611/t20061110_37960.htm.

[49] National Development and Reform Commission of the People's Republic of China, 'The 11th Five-Year Plan: Targets, Paths and Policy Orientation', 19 March 2006, http://en.ndrc.gov.cn/newsrelease/200603/t20060323_63813.html.

[50] Krekel, Adams and Bakos, 'Occupying the Information High Ground', p. 68.

[51] Dennis J. Blasko, 'Chinese Strategic Thinking: People's War in the 21st Century', *China Brief*, vol. 10, no. 6, 18 March 2010.

CHAPTER FOUR

Battle for the Soul of the Internet

Just as cyber policy lies at the heart of China's domestic-reform agenda, so too has it begun to influence fundamentally the state's approach to foreign policy and international security. For China, an awareness of the risks posed by the cyber domain has deepened an ingrained sense of insecurity – a sense that to outside observers seems at odds with the country's economic power, growing military capacity and general aura of stability. Since the era of reform and opening up that began in the late 1970s, China has seen a peaceful international environment as essential to economic modernisation. And, now that the cyber domain has become the principal vector for the next phase of this modernisation process, the country's leaders have seized on the importance of securing a global cyber environment that facilitates their domestic agenda and minimises external threats. International debates on global cyber governance and cyber security have become key battlegrounds for China. There, Beijing has become aware of its increasing strength and influence, while retaining a strong perception of threat, and has exchanged a largely reactive approach for one that is more proactive, focusing ever more on strategic opportunities within the cyber domain.

China's emerging position on global cyber governance and security forms part of a wider shift in a foreign policy that between the late 1970s and 2008 was largely conspicuous by its absence, at least in terms of its external impact. The country has always jealously guarded what it regarded as its core interests abroad, but since the 1949 founding of the People's Republic such interests have been few, and have required little more than a border-management policy. China's foreign policy was therefore focused almost exclusively on creating a favourable international environment for economic reform and opening up. This non-assertive approach was reinforced by the international response to the government crackdown in Tiananmen Square, which gave rise to Deng Xiaoping's '24-character strategy', referred to in the Western media as 'hide and bide' (see Introduction). In the ensuing period, China's approach to foreign policy underwent a series of modifications. Building on the Five Principles of Peaceful Coexistence, the cornerstone of that policy since the time of Mao Zedong, the Chinese leadership introduced several measures. The first of these was the New Security Concept, which argued for a change from a zero-sum approach to international security to one based on greater mutuality.[1] This was followed by President Jiang Zemin's 'period of strategic opportunity', an idea that was announced in his 2002 report to the 16th Party Congress, and that identified the first two decades of the twenty-first century as a period of peace and stability during which China could concentrate on economic development.[2] The leadership then promoted the concept of *zhongguo heping jueqi* (China's peaceful rise), which was first advanced by Zheng Bijian, former vice-principal of the Central Party School, at the 2003 Boao Forum. According to this notion, China's ascent would not undermine the established international order, in contrast to that of other major geopolitical powers over the course of history.[3] New president Hu Jintao modified the concept to *zhongguo heping fazhan* (China's peaceful development) in 2004, and introduced the idea of the harmonious world the following year, at the United Nations' 60th Anniversary Summit.[4] And when other countries began to express concern about its growing military power, China referred to the importance of avoiding the 'Thucydides Trap' – a reference to the Athenian historian's explanation of the origin of the Peloponnesian War: 'it was the rise of Athens, and the fear that this inspired in Sparta, that made war inevitable.'[5]

During this period, Chinese diplomacy was still characterised by a reluctance to take hard decisions, a readiness to free-ride on US-supplied global security and a disinclination to challenge or confront Washington. (The latter was arguably made easier by the fact that the United States was distracted by its campaign against al-Qaeda after 9/11, and by the instability that followed the 2003 invasion of Iraq.) China sought to promote a 'good neighbours' policy, seeking to resolve territorial disputes with the countries on its periphery and promoting the concept of the joint exploitation of resources in areas of the South China Sea claimed by Southeast Asian states. And, as its vertiginous export-led economic growth generated an ever greater need for energy and raw materials, China rapidly expanded its global footprint, particularly in sub-Saharan Africa and Latin America. The country also modernised and expanded its diplomatic service, and made a conscious effort to invest in the projection of 'soft power', with a focus on the developing world.[6]

At the same time, other states in the Asia-Pacific became concerned by growing evidence of China's investment in military modernisation, and many embarked on their own such programmes while strengthening their bilateral relationships with Washington. Fearing strategic encirclement and lacking natural allies, China decried this turn to the US as redolent of outdated Cold War thinking. Beijing's relationship with Washington in particular became infinitely more complex in the early years of the new millennium. China's economic expansion during the 1990s enabled the US to benefit from a flood of cheap imports and money, as Chinese leaders invested a significant proportion of export earnings in US Treasury bonds. The scale of this investment was such that in 2007 US presidential candidate Hillary Clinton responded to a question from a constituent about the loss of US manufacturing jobs to China by asking 'how do you get tough on your banker?'.[7] Nonetheless, Beijing increasingly saw its dependence on US treasuries as a vulnerability, a perception that only increased when the 2008 financial crisis erupted. For Chinese leaders, the event was a moment of epiphany, shattering whatever faith they may have had in the Washington Consensus. The crisis cost China tens of millions of jobs, caused entire cities to lose their economic *raison d'être* and forced the government to launch a US$586 billion stimulus package to deal with the immediate fallout. Adding insult to injury, some of the Western countries most affected by the crisis asked China to assist them with increased imports and foreign direct investment.[8] The event also fuelled a widespread, if not universal, perception within Chinese foreign- and defence-policy circles of the US as a power in decline.

The crisis has been seen by many Western analysts as a catalyst for China's adoption of a much more strident and assertive foreign policy, leading to suggestions that the era of 'hide and bide' is coming to an end.[9] Numerous examples have been cited, starting with the forceful Chinese response to US President Barack Obama's 2009 decision to provide updated military equipment to Taiwan – and extending to Beijing's strategy, first implemented in 2014, of building permanent facilities with unmistakable military applications on features in the South China Sea. Whether this shift was long planned or simply the inevitable outcome of a changing balance of power is a moot point. Analysis of the issue is complicated by the inherent opacity of the Chinese decision-making process, and by China's unwillingness or inability to explain itself adequately to foreign powers – a quality apparent throughout its history. It is also arguably the case that China has struggled to adapt to a world in which it has so rapidly acquired a range of global interests. One leading Chinese foreign-policy specialist has likened the country to a gawky adolescent whose sudden increase in physical strength has not yet been moderated by a commensurate development in emotional maturity or judgement.[10]

Historically, beneath much Western analysis of China's posture lay a presumption that, as the country modernised economically, the leadership would face irresistible pressure for political reform from a rising middle class. And, to be fair to such analysis, this debate continues to run in China, with then-premier Wen Jiabao speaking in 2010 of the necessity of such reform.[11] But even as Wen made his case, Hu was moving towards a focus on greater ideological orthodoxy. And in 2013, when Xi Jinping replaced Hu as leader, it rapidly became evident that economic liberalisation might in theory be on the agenda, but political reform – at least, in terms of a move towards Western-style multi-party democracy – was out of the question, as reflected in the publication of Document Number 9 (see Chapter One). Under Xi, the leitmotifs of foreign policy have become the 'Chinese Dream' – a concept that envisages China as enjoying stability and prosperity, but also international respect – and the idea of a 'new kind of great power relationship' with Washington. Xi sought to promote the latter concept at both his 2013 summit with Obama in Sunnylands, and during his 2015 state visit to the US.[12] This is not, in fact, a new notion, but has formed the basis for Sino-Russian relations since the break-up of the Soviet Union. It can be boiled down to: acceptance of the reality of a multipolar world; recognition of spheres of influence; deference to UN authority; accommodation of core interests; enhanced cooperation; and implementation of the New Security Concept, which effectively subordinates customary international law to national interests.[13] Unsurprisingly, Washington's response to this concept has been determinedly non-committal. Long regarded as a status quo power, China is now beginning to show its aspirations to modify the post-war global security order in ways that accommodate its interests. In contrast to the US, China has never sought to impose its values or ideology on others and asks only that other nations respect its choices. Yet China's growing global power increases the likelihood that some of these values will acquire greater normative effect, and that those who oppose them will be subjected to coercion.

Since Xi's appointment as leader, there has also been an intensification of the internal rhetoric of external threat ever present in Marxist–Leninist discourse – to the extent that new references to *guowai didui shili* (foreign hostile forces) are published in the journals of the Chinese Communist Party and the People's Liberation Army (PLA) almost every day. Although Chinese leaders have long been aware of the internet's potential for subversion, their concerns were greatly amplified in the late 2000s by a series of 'colour revolutions' (a term borrowed from the Russian government) to varying degrees enabled and facilitated by information and communications technologies (ICTs).[14] The *People's Liberation Army Daily* published in August 2009 an op-ed entitled 'Internet Subversion: The Security Threat that Cannot Be Underplayed', which observed that:

the West enjoyed total dominance over the internet due to its ownership of the majority of hardware and software; the West sought to use the internet to spread subversion and promote its world view; the failed 2009 colour revolution in Moldova was largely instigated via Twitter and Facebook, as was Iran's Green Revolution of the same year; and, after achieving dominance in the naval, air and space domains, the US was seeking to replicate this success in cyberspace, as evidenced by its establishment of the Cyber Command.[15] Articles combining the themes of internet subversion and *guowai didui shili* appeared regularly throughout 2015 – a case in point being a commentary published in July in the Party's *Red Flag*, which observed that 'ideological interference in the internet by foreign hostile forces has increased in intensity. The internet has already established itself as the main front for such forces to undertake ideological subversion of our country.'[16]

Taken in isolation, the relentless escalation in rhetoric would seem to suggest that China's leadership has been moving towards an ever more xenophobic and confrontational mindset, reflecting an attitude that is undoubtedly widespread within China's military and security establishments. This apparent trend has led some scholars to speculate that the country may be on its way to becoming a garrison state.[17] However, such remarks need to be set in context: under Xi, the Party has driven to reinforce ideological conformity and loyalty among its membership (the real audience for the narrative), and to remind the PLA that its primary loyalty is to the Party. Indeed, Xi had emphasised this message to the military at the November 2014 Gutian Conference (see Chapter Three).[18] It is perhaps unsurprising that, having been born in a conspiratorial atmosphere, the Party should feel compelled to nurture a continued perception of external threat. To a degree, this arguably resembles the tendency of the US to define itself strategically in terms of a main enemy. And, in the Information Age, a view of conflict and contestation between states as a permanent feature of the international landscape is far from unique to a Marxist–Leninist political culture.

In this sense, the advent of the Information Age has arguably changed quite fundamentally the international terms of trade. This is particularly true in relation to international negotiations on internet governance and cyber security. For China, such negotiations provide an opportunity to erode the first-mover advantage of the US and its main Western allies, and to establish international regimes that provide China with a greater sense of security and influence. In effect, Beijing engages in these discussions to shape the strategic environment, including the PLA's potential battlespace, by limiting its adversaries' influence and room for manoeuvre (see Chapter Three). In pursuit of these objectives, China has skilfully enlisted the support of many states from the developing world by providing them with telecommunications infrastructure, and by employing the narrative that unequal cyber capabilities exacerbate the North–South imbalance.

Cyber governance and cyber security: new global battlegrounds

International concerns about internet governance first became manifest in the 1990s, as more and more countries connected to the internet. A particular cause of anxiety was the management of the domain-name system (DNS), which is in effect the global address book for the internet. Every computer online has a unique internet-protocol number that enables it to send and receive information, and to access all other computers connected to the internet. Since these numbers are too long to remember, they are simplified into addresses such as www.iiss. org. The top-level domains that appear at the end of an internet address are assigned to countries, such as .uk or .cn, or are generic designations such as .com, .org or .edu. The DNS is a distributed set of databases that is stored in computers around the world, and that contains the address numbers mapped to their corresponding domain names. These computers, known as root servers, must be coordinated to ensure connectivity across the internet.[19] The DNS had evolved in an ad hoc, organic manner, and was entirely American in both concept and execution. As was argued by Pekka Tarjanne, former secretary-general of the International Telecommunication Union (ITU), global internet governance was dependent on the goodwill of a small number of people who were engaged in the task only by historical accident; domain names were allocated on a monopoly basis; and the overall system was dominated by the US, and lacked a formal structure and legitimacy.[20] The administration of US President Bill Clinton, which regarded internet governance as outside the ITU's remit, responded to this criticism by founding in 1998 the Internet Corporation for Assigned Names and Numbers (ICANN), a California-based non-profit organisation that answered to the US Department of Commerce.

Washington had originally intended to allow ICANN to become a private entity within two years of its establishment, but changed its stance after 9/11, declaring the internet to be infrastructure critical to US security. Since then, the organisation's original structure has essentially persisted. Many states, including China, feared that Washington would use its position to exclude their top-level domains from the root servers, cutting them off from the internet altogether – although in practice that threat, to the extent that it was ever real, has been addressed by ICANN's extension of root-server functionality to countries other than the US, including China. Non-governmental entities such as the Internet Society and the Internet Engineering Task

Force shared the concerns of these states. These organisations, together with other non-state actors, have been important components of the multi-stakeholder system, a relatively loose and informal set of arrangements that enable the internet to function in a stable, predictable manner.

The first globally coordinated effort to address the issue of internet governance was the World Summit on the Information Society (WSIS), convened by the UN in December 2003 in Geneva. At that summit, Beijing took the initiative by proposing the negotiation of an international internet treaty and the establishment of an international internet organisation. Supported by many other G77 developing countries, China argued that internet governance covered all public-policy issues (including e-commerce and cyber crime), that the ITU should have an enhanced role and that all states should accept the principle of government leadership. The Chinese position was set out in a WSIS preparatory meeting led by Ambassador Sha Zukang, who stated that countries with different social systems and cultural traditions would handle the transition to the information society differently; information infrastructure would be the foundation of future economic progress, but was weak in developing countries; managing the transition would demand policy responses across a broad front, in line with national conditions; the security of the state would be a high priority; developed countries had an obligation to transfer resources and provide training to developing nations; and the private sector and civil society would be important drivers of change, but governments should take the lead in framing international responses.[21] The US and its allies – known informally as the 'like-minded' – were reluctant make changes to the multi-stakeholder approach or to concede a greater role in internet governance to the UN. The Declaration of Principles agreed at the end of the summit broadly reflected that position. For the US and its allies, the key issues were the stability of global connectivity and the free flow of information. The arrangements spawned by the WSIS, the Working Group on Internet Governance and the Internet Global Forum made little progress in bridging the divides exposed at the December 2003 summit, although the former reached the conclusion that the internet's complexity was such that it should not be governed by a single entity.

The next major event in the history of internet governance was the meeting of the ITU's World Conference on International Telecommunications (WCIT) in Dubai in December 2012. The rationale for the WCIT was that there was a need to revise the International Telecommunications Regulations (ITRs). These regulations created a framework for cooperation to ensure the global inter-operability of telecommunications – involving tasks such as the allocation of radio frequencies – and had not been revised since 1988, before the internet had become a global phenomenon. The event became highly politicised, with many civil-society groups portraying it as an attempt by authoritarian states to impose a global agenda of top-down government control that would inhibit the freedom of information flows.[22] There, the like-minded countries were again ranged against states such as China and Russia, with many members of the G77 favouring the position of Moscow and Beijing; 55 nations, most of them liberal democracies, rejected the proposed new ITRs on the grounds that they would create a new international regulatory regime for the internet and expand the powers of the ITU. However, 87 states signed the new ITRs. At the follow-up ITU Plenipotentiary Conference, held in Busan in 2014, the attendees decided not to afford the ITU an expanded role in internet governance. The same year, the NETmundial Initiative hosted by the Brazilian government made no progress in reaching a global consensus. And Russia refused to associate itself with that event's final Multistakeholder Statement on the grounds that the document did not seek to control national-security entities' collection of information on the citizens of other countries – a reaction to the revelations about US covert intelligence practices made by rogue National Security Agency (NSA) contractor Edward Snowden. China, in contrast, approved the statement.

However, China has not changed its basic position that national governments should have a greater say in global internet governance. Lu Wei, director of the Cyberspace Administration of China (CAC), published in December 2014 an article in which he made clear that the country preferred the 'multilateral' model of internet governance to the multi-stakeholder approach, arguing that

> with regard to the cyberspace governance, the U.S. advocates 'multi-stakeholders' while China believes in 'multilateral'. ['Multi-stakeholder' refers to all internet participants on an equal footing making the rules and is considered more 'people-centered' while 'multilateral' refers to the state making the rules based on the idea of the sovereignty of the nation-state representing its citizens.][23]

China has continually called for ICANN to become a genuinely independent international body. And the arrangements set out for the ICANN conference in Marrakech in March 2016, although not yet agreed at the time of writing, looked set to end the US Department of Commerce's oversight of the organisation, in line with Chinese interests. Beijing has stepped up its engagement in such meetings at every level, in a policy that amounts to the swarming of the global-governance agenda. A case in point was a 2015 meeting of the Internet Engineering

Task Force to which most Western countries sent one or two delegates while China sent 40.

Beijing also marked out its territory by convening in November 2014 the World Internet Conference (WIC) in Wuzhen, a Zhejiang canal town that was the birthplace of novelist and former People's Republic of China minister of culture Shen Dehong, better known by his pen name, Mao Dun. Serving almost as an international launch for Lu's new role as director of the CAC, the WIC appeared to be designed as a counterweight to the Western-dominated Global Conference on Cyberspace, begun in 2011 by the British government, with subsequent iterations held in Budapest, Seoul and The Hague. In the run-up to and during the WIC, Lu was unapologetic in emphasising that China would implement its own rules in the cyber domain, which included monitoring and filtering online content, and that any foreign entity wishing to do business there would need to abide by those rules. At a speech at the World Economic Forum's September 2014 meeting in Tianjin, Lu said that 'freedom and order are twin sisters, and they must live together. The same principle applies to security internationally. So we must have public order. And this public order cannot impact any particular local order.' He also likened the internet to a car that had to have brakes. In a press conference in preparation for the WIC, Lu stressed China's significant potential as a digital marketplace.[24]

Many Western states sent only low-ranking officials to Tianjin – European countries did so to signal their dissatisfaction with China's proposed legislation on ICT indigenisation in the banking sector – and few chief executive officers of major Western technology companies participated in the event. The organisers of the conference caused some controversy by slipping a draft final declaration under delegates' hotel-room doors at 11.00pm on the final night, with a request for comments and amendments by 8.00am the following day. One section of the draft referred to the need to respect the 'Internet sovereignty of all countries. We should respect each country's rights to the development, use and governance of the Internet, refrain from abusing resources and technological strengths to violate other countries' Internet sovereignty, and build an Internet order to equality and mutual benefit.' The draft also called for tighter restrictions on internet pornography and for the destruction of 'all dissemination channels of information of violent terrorism'[25] – the latter statement reflecting a Chinese diplomatic initiative to secure international acceptance of the need to address cyber terrorism as a discrete phenomenon. The draft was withdrawn due to multiple protests from delegates, a development that may have drawn a wry smile from China's professional diplomats, who appeared to have had no hand in organising the event. The mistake of issuing a draft is unlikely to be repeated. But China clearly intends to use the WIC as a mechanism for effecting changes in the international system for cyber governance. In his keynote address to the second such meeting, held in Wuzhen during 16–18 December 2015, President Xi spoke of the need for a 'multilateral, democratic and transparent global Internet governance system' while observing that 'existing rules governing cyberspace hardly reflect the desires and interests of the majority of countries'.[26] China, together with Russia and other members of the Shanghai Cooperation Organisation, inserted into the final declaration of the WSIS+10 conference held in New York during the same period a reference to global cyber governance as including multilateral processes, although this was followed by language referring to 'transparent, democratic and multi-stakeholder processes'.[27] Xi's remarks at the second WIC were followed by articles in the *Guangming Daily* and the *People's Daily* emphasising China's intention energetically to promote its vision for global internet governance.[28]

Substantive international discussions on global cyber security have progressed more slowly than those on global internet governance, despite the fact that the concerns that prompted them emerged at the same time. And the like-minded states have continuously sought to keep the two issues separate, although in practice that position is becoming increasingly unrealistic. Cyber security encompasses a broad agenda, but at the international level it focuses on actual or potential uses of ICTs that are incompatible with international peace and security. Specific issues include definitions of, and thresholds for, cyber attacks that would amount to an armed attack or use of force under Article 2(4) of the UN Charter; the applicability of international law to the deployment of military cyber capabilities; countries' use of non-state proxies to pursue political or military objectives in the cyber domain; and the employment of ICTs in inter-state conflict.[29]

Russia first raised the issue of international cyber security in September 1998, when then-foreign minister Igor Ivanov wrote to the UN secretary-general highlighting the risk that ICT developments might be used for purposes incompatible with the aims of the UN charter:

> We cannot permit the emergence of a fundamentally new area of international confrontation which may lead to an escalation of the arms race based on the latest developments of the scientific and technological revolution … I am referring to the creation of information weapons and the threat of information wars, which we understand as actions taken by one country to damage the information resources and systems of another country while at the same time protecting its own infrastructure.

Ivanov went on to propose that international information security be taken up as a topic of substantive discussion at the UN.[30] His letter resulted in a UN General Assembly resolution inviting the reaction of states, which exposed the deep ideological divide between the like-minded, which dominated in the use of ICTs, and authoritarian countries, which were deeply distrustful of this dominance and fearful of the vulnerabilities it created for their regimes. Cuba summed up the position of the latter group, highlighting the fact that Washington's pre-eminent position enabled it to impose technological standards that facilitated the use of ICTs as a means of aggression. Havana's comments reflected the reality that developing countries had no choice but to adopt these technologies, often without under-standing the risks involved or the vulnerabilities this created.[31] Such remarks proved prophetic in June 2013, when Snowden revealed US intelligence agencies' broad capacity to access the information networks of other states.

This initial foray into international cyber security drew up the dividing lines that have characterised the debate ever since, and that have turned international discussions on the issue into a strategic contest. Russia's approach to international cyber security is rooted in traditional concepts of information warfare, an activity that it sees as taking place at all times rather than just during periods of kinetic warfare. Within this concept, information is seen as a weapon that needs to be controlled, and key to achieving this is the ability to secure one's national information space to prevent hostile narratives from influencing the population. Within Russia – and China, which has been strongly influenced by Soviet doctrine – such perceptions have only been reinforced by the view of the role played by externally generated information in bringing an end first to the Cold War then to the Soviet Union. For states such as Russia and China, shaping the international agenda on cyber security – or information security, as they prefer to call it – is vital to shaping the battlespace.[32] And a significant part of that agenda is eroding the advantage enjoyed by potential adversaries, particularly the US. In that context, it is important to note that the architect of Russia's Information Security Doctrine, approved by President Vladimir Putin in 2000, is Colonel-General Vladislav Sherstyuk, a signals-intelligence officer in first the KGB and then its successor, the Federal Agency for Government Communications and Information.[33] In contrast, the like-minded states have been reluctant to acknowledge the validity of information security as a concept, fearing that any such concession would erode the ideal of free information flows, which they see as one of the key benefits of the internet. Instead, the US and its allies prefer to focus on technical issues of network integrity and hygiene.

Russian persistence resulted in 2004 in the first meeting of the UN Group of Governmental Experts on Developments in the Field of Information and Telecommunications in the Context of International Security (UN/GGE), convened under the UN First Committee. The first UN/GGE meeting served to highlight countries' fundamental differences in perception. The US made clear its objections to the proposition that states should have an internationally sanctioned right to control or filter content. In response to Russia's demand that countries address new threats posed by state exploitation of ICTs for military or national-security purposes, Washington stated that the 'law of armed conflict and its principles of necessity and proportionality and limitation of collateral damage already govern the use of such technologies'.[34] China continued to insist that the free flow of information should be conditioned by the need to safeguard national sovereignty and security, emphasising that there was a need to respect the historical, cultural and political differences between states.[35]

By 2009, when the next iteration of the UN/GGE met, some of the fears about states' use of cyber capabilities for coercive purposes had been realised, following attacks in Estonia, Georgia and Lithuania – all of which, ironically, the victims attributed to the Russian state or its proxies. Furthermore, the US had announced that it was setting up the Cyber Command. The second UN/GGE meeting recommended the implementation of four measures: a dialogue on norms of conduct for states' use of ICTs, with the aim of reducing risk and protecting critical infrastructure; confidence-building and risk-reduction exercises, including discussion of the use of ICTs in conflict; information exchange on national legislation and ICT security strategies, policies and technologies; and capacity-building in developing nations, and the elaboration of common terms and definitions of information security.[36]

The report created a sufficient basis for a third iteration of the group, whose meetings in 2012–13 led to a consensus. This involved a compromise whereby Russia and China accepted the proposition that 'international law, and in particular the charter of the United Nations, is applicable and is essential to maintaining peace and stability and promoting an open, secure, peaceful and accessible ICT environment', thereby meeting a condition set by the like-minded; and the like-minded agreed to the proposition that 'State sovereignty and international norms and principles that flow from sovereignty apply to State conduct of ICT-related activities, and to their jurisdiction over ICT infrastructure within their territory', which satisfied a major Russian and Chinese concern.[37] Together with Belarus, Malaysia, Pakistan and Egypt, China and Russia also sought to avoid any inclusion in the UN/GGE text of states' right to self-defence within the cyber domain, and were resistant to adding language that referred to International Humanitarian Law. This reflects the well-established Chinese position that any such acknowledgement would be tantamount to accepting that cyberspace is a domain of conflict. To Beijing's approval, the report also recommended a series of voluntary, non-binding norms of conduct:

> states should not knowingly allow their territory to be used for internationally wrongful acts using ICTs; states should not conduct or knowingly support ICT activity that intentionally damages critical infrastructure; states should take steps to ensure supply chain security, and should seek to prevent the proliferation of malicious ICT and the use of harmful hidden functions; states should not conduct or knowingly support activity to harm the information systems of another state's [computer emergency response teams] and should not use their own teams for malicious international activity; [and] states should respect the UN resolutions that are linked to human rights on the internet and to the right to privacy in the digital age.[38]

The norms relating to critical infrastructure, computer emergency response teams and supply chains reflected long-standing US preoccupations, and their inclusion was hence something of a tactical victory for the like-minded. But China is equally interested in the development of measures to ensure the stability of global supply chains, which it sees as integral to its long-term economic-development plans.[39] The UN/GGE serves as a reminder that Russia's cyber-security strategy is increasingly a reflection of its more confrontational relationship with NATO and the West, and less concerned with global connectivity. In contrast, China's interest in global connectivity makes it more prone to compromise with the like-minded. Indeed, diplomats attending the 2015 UN/GGE commented on the difficulty Russia experienced gaining China's approval for some of its positions.

Beijing remains wedded to the International Code of Conduct for Information Security, an initiative begun in 2011, when Russia, also supported by Tajikistan and Uzbekistan, circulated a draft of the proposal at the UN. The document seeks to, inter alia, proscribe states' use of cyber weapons and enshrine their right to control internet content. China described the draft Code as raising

> a series of basic principles of maintaining information and network security which cover the political, military, economic, social, cultural, technical and other aspects. The principles stipulate that countries shall not use such information and telecom technologies as the network to conduct hostile behaviours and acts of aggression or to threaten international peace and security and stress that countries have the rights and obligations to protect their information and cyberspace as well as key information and network infrastructure from threats, interference and sabotage attacks.[40]

The authors of the Code of Conduct circulated a new version in 2015,[41] prior to which China actively lobbied the like-minded to support the document. The new iteration reflects norm-building activities conducted within the framework of the Shanghai Cooperation Organisation, and takes account of major developments since 2011 such as the WCIT, the Snowden revelations and the US–China slanging match on the subject of state-sponsored cyber industrial espionage (the latter has plagued the bilateral relationship for most of the last decade). The draft recognises the work of the UN/GGE; puts great emphasis on the rights of states in matters of digital public policy, and on the concept of cyber sovereignty; and highlights the issues of digital inequalities between states, as well as the threats to national security posed by some nations' dominant positions (the latter calculated to resonate with many G77 countries). The draft Code of Conduct includes little discussion of human rights, beyond a few references to the International Covenant on Civil and Political Rights. As a result, Western civil-society groups have expressed concern that the adoption of the Code would enable states to subordinate universal human rights to state laws and the dictates of what China refers to as 'diversity', meaning the acceptance of different political and cultural traditions.[42] The Code is best seen as a part of a diplomatic war of attrition in which states such as China and Russia refer to the draft as though it reflected established global norms, while seeking to recruit other countries to their cause. The approach has arguably proven successful: the like-minded have struggled to come up with a persuasive counter-narrative, and hence risk being seen as adopting a negative approach to what are presented as unexceptionable proposals, and of acting purely out of desire to maintain their dominant status. Chinese diplomats have also begun to broaden support for their position by introducing cyber-security issues into other fora, such as the UN Fourth Committee, which deals with issues such as human rights and peacekeeping.

Snowden revelations and Chinese cyber espionage

Snowden's revelations have had a major impact on China's international agenda. The information he initially leaked about the NSA's bulk collection programmes – which, from the outset, Western media outlets mischaracterised as 'mass surveillance' – coincided with the Sunnylands summit, at which Obama attempted to address the issue of state-sponsored cyber industrial espionage, reportedly showing Xi specific evidence of

China's theft of US intellectual property.[43] This initiative elicited no substantive response and, a few days later, Snowden, then in Hong Kong, revealed that the NSA had collected large quantities of Chinese text messages and had also penetrated the networks of Tsinghua University, a major centre of Chinese cyber research.[44] China's mass media gave prominent coverage to the revelations, and *lengjingmen* (PRISM-gate, a reference to a major NSA data-collection programme) gained widespread currency within the country. Chinese officials were initially more circumspect in commenting on the Snowden revelations, at least in terms of specific references to the US, no doubt calculating they spoke for themselves in substantiating Beijing's established narrative of American cyber hegemony around the globe.

But the gloves came off in May 2014, after the US Department of Justice indicted five officers in the Shanghai-based Unit 61398, part of China's signals-intelligence agency, the Third Department of the PLA General Staff.[45] China's Internet Media Research Center published on 26 May 2014 a report entitled 'The United States' Global Surveillance Record', setting out the Snowden revelations in exhaustive, misleading detail, and concluding that

> such activities have gone way beyond the imperatives of the counter-terrorism agenda and have demonstrated the ugly face of a country that is prepared to put aside morality in pursuit of its own interests. Such activity is a flagrant violation of international law, is a serious infringement of human rights and substantially harms global security.[46]

State news agency Xinhua published in February 2015 an article entitled 'The USA Talks of Cyber Security and the World Laughs'. One of several cartoons in the piece shows an Uncle

Sam figure connected to cables wrapping around the planet, while Putin and German Chancellor Angela Merkel look on, beneath the caption 'The USA and UK Hack the Keys to SIM Cards'. Below this is an image of President Obama smiling and wearing a pair of headphones, above two photographs of the NSA's headquarters in Fort Meade. The article largely repeats the key point in the Internet Media Research Center report.[47] References to the Snowden revelations – typically attributed to *gebie de guojia* (a particular country) – are now a standard feature of China's diplomatic discussions with Western states, and Beijing undoubtedly sees them as providing a useful counterweight to the US allegations of Chinese state-sponsored cyber industrial espionage.

Meanwhile, China has continued to develop a series of bilateral efforts to supplement its promotion of multilateral cyber diplomacy. These activities include Track 1 and Track 1.5 cyber-security dialogues with the US, the United Kingdom, the European Union and Australia, although the Track 1 dialogue with the US was suspended following the indictment of the PLA officers. The Track 1.5 dialogues provide an opportunity to explore other parties' positions without making commitments, and to clarify their policies and practices – although they are unlikely to generate any major breakthroughs in and of themselves. Beijing has also signed a bilateral agreement on international information security with Moscow, one of several deals made during Xi's May 2015 visit to Russia. This agreement is probably more valuable to Putin as Russia endures diplomatic isolation and economic sanctions from the West in relation to the war in eastern Ukraine, and it expands on concepts developed under the Shanghai Cooperation Organisation. The deal commits both countries to opposing a range of threats, including the use of technology to 'carry out acts of aggression aimed at the violation sovereignty, security and territorial integrity of states'; 'interfere in the internal affairs of states'; cause economic damage; or commit crimes such as data breaches for terrorist purposes or to disseminate information that 'harms political and socio-economic systems, or the spiritual, moral and cultural environment of other states'. Under the agreement, China and Russia will increase the quantities of cyber-security technology they share and will collaborate against crime and terrorism, while working to promote 'norms of international law in order to ensure national and international information security'.[48] Concerns that this agreement might represent a cyber alliance against the US are almost certainly misplaced. While China and Russia share important aims in cyber governance and security, levels of strategic trust between them remain far below that which has facilitated the Five Eyes intelligence alliance (between Australia, Canada, New Zealand, the UK and the US).

Possibly a more significant development in China's bilateral cyber diplomacy occurred during President Xi's September 2015 state visit to the US. The trip underlined the unique aspects of Sino-US relations in the cyber domain. Xi's first port of call was Seattle where he attended, inter alia, a round-table discussion with 30 US and Chinese business leaders, most of them from the ICT sector. While the event proved to be little more than a photo opportunity, Beijing told the US companies involved that their business prospects in China would suffer if their chief executive officers did not attend – a timely reminder of the country's economic leverage, and the stark instrumentality with which Chinese leaders are prepared to exercise it.[50] However, the most significant product of the visit was an agreement on cyber security (see box 'US–China agreement on cyber security').

Critics of the deal have dismissed it as a pro forma exercise. But the measured diplomatic language of the document

US–China agreement on cyber security

'The United States and China agree that timely responses should be provided to requests for information and assistance concerning malicious cyber activities. Further, both sides agree to cooperate, in a manner consistent with their respective national laws and relevant international obligations, with requests to investigate cybercrimes, collect electronic evidence, and mitigate malicious cyber activity emanating from their territory. Both sides also agree to provide updates on the status and results of those investigations to the other side, as appropriate.

The United States and China agree that neither country's government will conduct or knowingly support cyber-enabled theft of intellectual property, including trade secrets or other confidential business information, with the intent of providing competitive advantages to companies or commercial sectors.

Both sides are committed to making common effort to further identify and promote appropriate norms of state behavior in cyberspace within the international community. The United States and China welcome the July 2015 report of the UN Group of Governmental Experts in the Field of Information and Telecommunications in the Context of International Security, which addresses norms of behavior and other crucial issues for international security in cyberspace. The two sides also agree to create a senior experts group for further discussions on this topic.

The United States and China agree to establish a high-level joint dialogue mechanism on fighting cybercrime and related issues. China will designate an official at the ministerial level to be the lead and the Ministry of Public Security, Ministry of State Security, Ministry of Justice, and the State Internet and Information Office will participate in the dialogue. The U.S. Secretary of Homeland Security and the U.S. Attorney General will co-chair the dialogue, with participation from representatives from the Federal Bureau of Investigation, the U.S. Intelligence Community and other agencies, for the US. This mechanism will be used to review the timeliness and quality of responses to requests for information and assistance with respect to malicious cyber activity of concern identified by either side. As part of this mechanism, both sides agree to establish a hotline for the escalation of issues that may arise in the course of responding to such requests. Finally, both sides agree that the first meeting of this dialogue will be held by the end of 2015, and will occur twice per year thereafter.'[49]

masked Washington's hard-edged response to Chinese cyber espionage (see Chapter Two). Following four days of meetings between US and Chinese security officials, Obama made clear that cyber industrial espionage was unacceptable, saying that 'there comes a point at which we consider this a core national security threat and will treat it as such'.[51] It remains to be seen how much practical impact the cyber-security agreement will have, but it may, in fact, sit well with the Chinese government's desire to tame China's lawless cyberspace, and could lead to a crackdown on some of the noisy, reduplicative non-state cyber exploitation that Beijing has tolerated. And, to the extent that China fails to comply with the agreement, the US may be able to recover some of the moral high ground it lost thanks to the Snowden revelations.

Long-term strategic contest

The cyber-security deal may help to draw some of the poison from Sino-American relations, which would be a victory for the US. However, it is unlikely to have much effect on the global struggle for strategic advantage between two value systems that appear hard to reconcile. For China, efforts to ensure social stability and national security take precedence over all else, and controlling access to information has been a part of that process since long before the founding of the People's Republic. To feel safe, China needs an international cyber environment that provides assurances in these areas, and it appears unwilling to compromise on the point.

Beijing has continued its patient diplomatic game to erode the US cyber advantage and to garner international support for its positions. At the same time, China has successfully held out to major US technology companies the beguiling prospect of access to the world's largest, fastest-growing market in digital goods and services – provided that these firms follow Chinese laws. Thus far, the evidence suggests that most companies will make the necessary concessions: LinkedIn has complied with Chinese government requests to censor data and Yahoo! has handed over emails. Apple has agreed to submit its products for Chinese audit and has begun storing iCloud data on Chinese users in encrypted servers in China (although the firm claims that the Chinese authorities do not have access to the relevant encryption other than through US legal processes).[52] The FBI has also alleged that the Chinese authorities requested data on around 4,000 iPhones in the first six months of 2015, and that Apple produced that data 74% of the time. The company said that the claim was based on 'thinly sourced news reports to inaccurately suggest that Apple had colluded with the Chinese government to undermine [iPhone] buyers' security'. But it did not expressly deny the FBI claim.[53] Facebook chief Mark Zuckerberg has engaged in a high-profile lobbying exercise with the Chinese leadership to gain access to the Chinese market. Meanwhile, US-based services such as Airbnb and Uber have ambitious plans for expanding in that market – although the latter admitted to losing US$1bn in China per year.[54]

China's ICT champions are becoming more extrovert and active in the international arena. Alibaba has hired a former Goldman Sachs executive to help reinforce its position in the US market, and has established bases in France and Germany. The Chinese equivalent of Uber, Didi Chuxing, has invested in similar services in the US, India and Singapore, and mobile-phone manufacturer Xiaomi is moving into India, Indonesia and Brazil.[55] Chinese private companies are also buying up small and medium-sized ICT companies in developed Western economies such as those of the UK and Germany. And China is seeking to shape the global telecommunications environment by setting technical standards for 4G and 5G networks, an aspiration that appears to enjoy the support of the ITU Secretary-General Houlin Zhao, a Chinese citizen who has accepted Beijing's recommendation to use the Chinese designation IMT–2020 for the 5G project.[56]

China is gaining significant political leverage through the activities of its telecommunications champions Huawei and ZTE, which between them have built major systems in around 30 African countries. These systems include networks for 3G and fibre-optic communications networks, as well as e-governance systems. Huawei has also established training centres in seven African states, a research and development facility in South Africa and a network-operations base in Cairo, and it has partnered with Microsoft in developing a low-cost smartphone for the African market. In many cases, Huawei and ZTE operate and maintain the infrastructure they built on behalf of local telecommunications companies. Chinese firms' success in challenging Western dominance in the African market derives from several factors: price competitiveness stemming from low-cost Chinese manufacturing, as well as the use of inexpensive sub-contractors to deal with the challenging aspects of infrastructure development; a greater appetite for risk than many of their Western counterparts; and significant support from the Chinese government, especially in the form of concessionary finance from the Export–Import Bank of China.[57]

This major incursion into Africa has its critics. The World Bank has condemned ZTE's contract with Ethiopia's Ethio Telecom as anti-competitive; Human Rights Watch has criticised Huawei and ZTE for providing monitoring equipment used to conduct surveillance on human-rights and civil-liberties activists across the continent; and many Africans have highlighted the use of Chinese workers rather than locals, as well as the negative impact on indigenous technical development caused by Chinese firms' provision of infrastructure (complaints that go far beyond the telecommunications sector). There is undoubtedly truth in all these points, but the fact remains that Huawei and ZTE have created substantial telecommunications infrastructure that otherwise would not exist, and which has enabled significant expansions in economic activity. It has also been suggested that China may exploit its control of African telecommunications infrastructure for intelligence-gathering purposes. There is no hard evidence to support this proposition, but it would scarcely be surprising if China were engaged in such activities, whether independently or in conjunction with the states concerned. Chinese engagement appears to have been translated into explicit political support for some of Beijing's policies, a notable example being the 2015 cyber-security pact between the Chinese and South African governments, which made reference to, inter alia, collaboration on information security.[58]

In short, China has shown patience and skill in using its economic weight and political influence to shape the international cyber-security and -governance agenda. While the country's policies and messaging on cyber sovereignty and a multilateral internet-governance model attract much pushback from Western liberal democracies, they find a more receptive audience in developing countries that share its resentment of perceived Western dominance in the cyber domain. For better or worse, China's positions are beginning to gain international traction, and to raise as yet unanswered questions about the possible emergence of two distinct, competing models for the future evolution of the internet. Policymakers in Western states are only now beginning to confront this possibility.

Notes

1 Anil Kumar, 'New Security Concept of China', Institute of Peace and Conflict Studies, May 2012.
2 Kerry Brown, 'Why 2016 Could Be a Nightmare for China', *Diplomat*, 27 January 2015.
3 'Zhongyang dangxiao yuan changwu fuxiaozhang zheng bijian: zhongguo heping jueqi xin daolu', *China News*, 22 March 2004, http://www.chinanews.com/n/2004-03-21/26/415936.html.
4 Hu Jintao, 'Build Towards a Harmonious World of Lasting Peace and Common Prosperity', 15 September 2005, http://www.un.org/webcast/summit2005/statements15/china050915eng.pdf.
5 Xi Jinping, 'Speech on China–US Relations', 22 September 2015, http://english.cri.cn/12394/2015/09/24/3746s897214.htm.
6 Carola McGiffert (ed.), *Chinese Soft Power and its Implications for the United States: Competition and Cooperation in the Developing World*, Center For Strategic and International Studies, March 2009.
7 Tom Curry, 'Clinton Sounds the China Alarm as '08 Issue', NBC, 3 February 2007.
8 'China 2008: The Global Financial Crisis', *China Digital Times*, 8 December 2008.
9 For a detailed analysis of Western and Chinese assessments of China's apparent change in approach, see Michael D. Swaine, 'Perceptions of an Assertive China', *China Leadership Monitor*, no. 32, May 2010.
10 Private communication.
11 Malcolm Moore, 'Wen Jiabao Promises Political Reform', *Telegraph*, 4 October 2010.
12 'New Type of Great Power Relations', CCTV, 20 September 2015.
13 Paul Mancinelli, 'Conceptualizing "New Type Great Power Relations": The Sino-Russian Model', *China Brief*, vol. 14, no. 9, May 2014.
14 Gideon Rachman, 'China's Strange Fear of a Colour Revolution', *Financial Times*, 9 February 2015.
15 'Wangluo dianfu: burong xiaoqu de anquan weixie', *China News*, 6 August 2009, www.chinanews.com.cn/cul/news/2009/08-06/1806701.shtml.
16 Li Yanyan, 'Ruhe kandai dangqian wangluo yishixingtai anquan de xingshi', *Red Flag*, 27 July 2015.
17 The concept of a garrison state was first evoked by US sociologist Harold Lasswell in a 1941 article in the *American Journal of Sociology*. The idea postulates a world in which states are dominated by elites who are specialists in violence. Harold D. Lasswell, 'The Garrison State', *American Journal of Sociology*, vol. 46, no. 4, January 1941, pp. 455–68.
18 James Mulvenon, 'Hotel Gutian: We Haven't Had That Spirit Here Since 1929', *Chinese Leadership Monitor*, no. 46, March 2015.
19 Lennard G. Kruger, 'Internet Governance and the Domain Name System: Issues for Congress', Congressional Research Service, 23 March 2016, http://www.fas.org/sgp/crs/misc/R42351.pdf.
20 Pekka Tarjanne, 'Internet Governance: Towards Voluntary Multilateralism', 29 April 1997, http://

www.itu.int/newsarchive/projects/dns-meet/KeynoteAddress.html.

21 Sha Zukang, 'Statement by Ambassador Sha Zukang, Head of the Chinese Delegation at the First Meeting of the Intergovernmental Preparatory Committee of the World Summit on the Information Society', 1 July 2002, http://www.fmprc.gov.cn/ce/cegv/eng/zmjg/jgthsm/t85538.htm.

22 IISS, 'Internet's Future on the Agenda at Dubai Meeting', *Strategic Comments*, no. 44, 2012.

23 Lu Wei, 'Cyber Sovereignty Must Rule Global Internet', *World Post*, 15 December 2014.

24 David Bandurski, 'Ali Baba's Cave and Pandora's Box', China Media Project, 5 November 2014.

25 Catherine Shu, 'China Tried to Get World Internet Conference Attendees to Ratify This Ridiculous Draft Declaration', *TechCrunch*, 20 November 2014.

26 'Xi Slams "Double Standards", Advocates Shared Future in Cyberspace', Xinhua, 16 December 2015.

27 http://digitalwatch.giplatform.org/instruments/wsis-10-resolution.

28 'Wangluo kongjian luanxiang huhuan zhuquan yuanze, qizhixianming changdao wangluo zhuquan', *Guangming Ribao*, 9 January 2016, http://media.people.co.cn/n1/2016/0109/c40606-28031880.html; 'Tuidong hulianwang quanqiu zhilitixi bian ge, jiji canyu guize zhiding', *People's Daily*, 12 January 2016, http://media.people.com.cn/n1/2016/0112/c40606-28039805.html.

29 IISS, *Evolution of the Cyber Domain: The Implications for National and Global Security* (Abingdon: Routledge, 2015).

30 Igor Ivanov, 'Letter Dated 23 September 1998 from the Permanent Representative of the Russian Federation to the United Nations Addressed to the Secretary-General', A/C.1/53/3, 30 September 1998.

31 UN General Assembly, 'Developments in the Field of Information and Telecommunications in the Context of International Security: Report of the Secretary-General', A/54/213, 10 August 1999.

32 See Timothy L. Thomas, 'Russian Information Warfare Theory: The Consequences of 2008', in Stephen J. Blank and Richard Weitz (eds), *The Russian Military Today and Tomorrow: Essays in Memory of Mary Fitzgerald* (Carlisle, PA: Strategic Studies Institute, 2010).

33 Andrei Soldatov and Irina Borogan, *The Red Web: The Struggle between Russia's Digital Dictators and the New Online Revolutionaries* (New York: Public Affairs, 2015) pp. 224–6.

34 Nicholas Tsagourias and Russell Buchan (eds), *Research Handbook on International Law and Cyberspace* (Cheltenham: Edward Elgar Publishing, 2015), pp. 474–5.

35 UN Office for Disarmament Affairs, 'Fact Sheet: Developments in the Field of Information and Telecommunications in the Context of International Security', January 2014, https://unoda-web.s3.amazonaws.com/wp-content/uploads/2014/01/Information-Security-Fact-Sheet-Jan-2014.pdf.

36 UN General Assembly, 'Report of the Group of Governmental

Experts on Developments in the Field of Information and Telecommunications in the Context of International Security: Report of the Secretary-General', A/65/201, 3 July 2011.

37 UN General Assembly, 'Report of the Group of Governmental Experts on Developments in the Field of Information and Telecommunications in the Context of International Security', 22 July 2015.

38 Ibid.

39 Private communication, September 2015.

40 Ministry of Foreign Affairs of the People's Republic of China, 'China, Russia and Other Countries Submit the Document of International Code of Conduct for Information Security to the United Nations', 13 September 2011, http://www.fmprc.gov.cn/mfa_eng/wjb_663304/zzjg_663340/jks_665232/jkxw_665234/t858978.shtml.

41 Liu Jieyi et al., 'Letter Dated 9 January from the Permanent Representatives of China, Kazakhstan, Kyrgyzstan, the Russian Federation, Tajikistan and Uzbekistan to the United Nations Addressed to the Secretary-General', A/69/723, 13 January 2015.

42 Sarah McKune, 'An Analysis of the International Code of Conduct for Information Security', Citizen Lab, 28 September 2015.

43 Bonnie Glaser and Jacqueline Vitello, 'US–China Relations: Sizing Each Other Up at Sunnylands', Comparative Connections, September 2013.

44 Luke Harding, The Snowden Files: The Inside Story of the World's Most Wanted Man (London: Faber and Faber, 2014), pp. 218–19.

45 US Department of Justice, 'U.S. Charges Five Chinese Military Hackers for Cyber Espionage against U.S. Corporations and a Labor Organization for Commercial Advantage', 19 May 2014.

46 Internet Media Research Center, 'The United States' Global Surveillance Record', 26 May 2014.

47 Huanqiu Lifangti, 'Meiguo ti wangluo anquan, quan shijie xiaole', Xinhua, 27 February 2015.

48 Alexandra Kulikova, 'China–Russia Cyber-Security Pact: Should the US Be Concerned?', Russia Direct, 21 May 2015.

49 White House, 'Fact Sheet: President Xi Jinping's State Visit to the United States', 25 September 2015.

50 Todd C. Frankel, 'No Soft Landing as Chinese President Xi Begins State Visit', Washington Post, 21 September 2015.

51 'US and China Officials Talk Cybersecurity after Obama's Warning about Attacks', Agence France-Presse, 13 September 2015.

52 Grant Gross, 'Report: Apple Agrees to Chinese Security Audits of Its Products', PC World, 23 January 2015.

53 'Apple Hits Back at "Corrosive" Claim by US Government', BBC, 11 March 2016.

54 'Uber Car-hire App Losing $1bn in China Every Year, Says CEO', BBC, 19 February 2016, http://www.bbc.co.uk/news/business-35610147.

55 Edward Tse and Matthias Hendrichs, 'Well Connected: The Growing Reach of China's Internet Sector', South China Morning Post, 3 January 2016.

56 Yu Dawei, 'China Sets Sights on Influencing 5G Standard', Caixin, 11 March 2015.

57 Andrea Marshall, 'China's Mighty Telecom Footprint in Africa', eLearning Africa, http://ela-newsportal.com/china%E2%80%99s-mighty-telecom-footprint-in-africa/.

58 Masa Kekana, 'Ministry Signs Pact with China on Cyber Security', Eyewitness News, 9 June 2015, http://ewn.co.za/2015/06/09/Telecommunication-ministry-signs-pact-with-China-on-cyber-security.

In the mid-nineteenth century, a China that had become isolated, complacent and self-referential was subjected to a rude awakening at the hands of Western powers imbued with a sense of cultural and moral superiority that mirrored the country's own. The resulting struggle for modernisation, and for a new identity that enabled China to retain a measure of cultural self-respect while becoming economically and technically competitive with the West, has been prolonged and painful. The lesson China's Communist leadership has drawn from this experience is stark and uncompromising: a state that is weak will be subjected to bullying and humiliation. And China's leaders are determined above all else to ensure that the country is never again humiliated. At the same time, the rise of the West and the decline of China fits into the conceptual framework of history as a cycle expressed in the opening line of the classic Ming dynasty novel *Sanguo Yanyi* (*Romance of Three Kingdoms*): 'it is said that when the state has long been united it is bound to become divided; and having long been divided is bound to become reunited.'[1] Within that framework, China's time has come (again) and the West's is in the process of waning. This may seem a simplistic notion, and there are many Chinese scholars who would dismiss it. But texts such as *Sanguo Yanyi* have shaped the collective Chinese psyche in much the same way that the Bible and the works of Shakespeare have shaped the thinking of the Anglophone world, and their impact cannot be brushed aside lightly.

One concomitant of China's sense of humiliation is a strongly held perception that the West has sought to deny the country access to much science and technology to preserve for itself a clear strategic advantage. This view combines with a conviction that the West's agenda is intrinsically hostile to communism, as evidenced by the triumphalism that attended the collapse of the Berlin Wall and the subsequent demise of the Soviet Union. While China's leaders harboured no illusions about the shortcomings of the Soviet system, they viewed the confusion and economic collapse that attended its downfall, and the consequent emergence of the United States as the unchallenged global superpower, as inherently undesirable and strategically destabilising. And they feared, as they still do, that they would be the West's next target.

This is the mindset against which one must evaluate China's policies and strategies. The cyber domain is an increasingly critical factor in the country's pursuit of strength through modernisation, and of protection from perceived threats, whether internal or external. Beijing sees cyberspace as crucial to the next phase of economic development, not only for realising the potential of the digital economy but also for developing the next generation of technologies, which will provide employment opportunities in the place of an industrial-era manufacturing sector progressively less able to do so. And, far beyond that, the Chinese leadership sees the cyber domain as having significant capacity to facilitate both governance and social control. For all the leadership's expressed concerns about external threats, what it fears most of all is the prospect of an irrecoverable breakdown of internal order. From this comes the imperative to develop e-governance as a way of showing responsiveness to public concerns, delivering effective services to the population and reducing the scope for corruption – the endemic nature of which the Chinese Communist Party now regards as an existential threat to its rule. This overriding concern with internal order also accounts for China's obses-sion with controlling and filtering online content, as well as for the efforts now under way to bring the rule of law – or, perhaps more correctly, 'rule by law' – to the chaotic Chinese cyber domain. Since the arrival of the internet in China, successive generations of Chinese leaders have taken what in their terms must have seemed big risks by actively promoting digitalisa-tion, and in so doing allowing far greater information flows and more freedom of expression than they desired. But it is now clear that, faced with a choice between freedom of expres-sion and social control, the Party will ultimately choose the latter. The Chinese state has devoted huge resources to moni-toring and managing internet content, particularly exchanges on social media, and the leadership appears confident that it has the technological edge needed to stay ahead of the curve. Beyond that, there are signs that the Party's propagandists and ideologues may be developing a vision for the Chinese cyber domain that enables it to exercise control over citizens by both filtering the information they access and compiling such detailed electronic data on individuals – including their entire browsing history and all their social-media posts – that any perceived infractions can be used as leverage against them.[2]

But, while seized of the criticality of the cyber domain to China's economic and social development, the leadership has an equally strong apprehension of the vulnerabilities arising from dependence on systems that have been developed and operated by Western corporations, largely in accordance with Western rules and values. And, as indicated by the revelations on US intelligence collection made by Edward Snowden, Chinese communications are open to interception by Washington and its allies to a greater degree than Beijing had realised. This perception of vulnerability has sparked efforts to promote indigenous innovation, designed to reduce China's dependence on Western technologies and networks. Most Chinese firms specialising in information and communications technologies (ICTs) are private rather than state-owned, and are showing a genuine capacity for innovation. But moving away from dependence on Western systems may take time, as suggested by China's decision to develop a secure government-communications system in cooperation with Microsoft.[3] More controversially, this sense of vulnerability has resulted in a spate of legislation that deals mostly with national-security issues and to varying degrees requires foreign ICT operators to make their source code and encrypted communications accessible to Chinese law-enforcement authorities. Supported by the US government, the companies concerned have pushed back against this series of laws, forcing the Chinese leadership into some tactical withdrawals. But the direction of travel is clear, and the head of the Cyberspace Administration of China has repeatedly said that foreign companies aspiring to work in the country will have to accept Chinese rules, including those on monitoring and filtering online content. And China is becoming increasingly confident that the gravitational attraction of the world's largest online user community and, potentially, its largest digital marketplace will overcome the reservations of major Western ICT firms.

The sense of insecurity driving China's domestic internet policy also shapes its cyber diplomacy, which has the overall objective of diminishing the West's first-mover advantage. In particular, China has sought to promote a model of internet governance that gives a decisive role to national governments under the aegis of the United Nations, a structure labelled 'multilateralism'. This arrangement resonates with the many G77 countries that share Beijing's reservations about US strategic pre-eminence, and that see the digital divide and Washington's domination of the cyber domain as perpetuating entrenched North–South inequalities. China is also acquiring political influence with these states by providing them with ICT networks on favourable terms. Similarly, in the international debate on cyber security conducted primarily through the United Nations Group of Governmental Experts, China has sought to promote the concept of cyber sovereignty – in effect, formal acknowledgement of states' right to determine what information passes through their national networks. This concept also resonates with countries in the developing world, many of which are indifferent to the West's focus on cyber security. In this context, China has taken every opportunity to highlight what it characterises as the United States' obsession with achieving absolute security at the expense of other states, through both the espionage programmes revealed by Snowden and the development of offensive military cyber capabilities that seek to exploit its first-mover advantage.

Meanwhile, China has not been slow to exploit its rapidly growing reach in the cyber domain in pursuit of national advantage, as suggested by its alleged sponsorship of large-scale cyber industrial espionage. While Beijing vigorously refutes these charges, Chinese securocrats privately admit that such activity is taking place, and is justified by China's national-security imperatives of economic development and social stability, as well as the West's continuing reluctance to share science and technology in an equitable manner. It is neither possible to measure how important such espionage has been in achieving China's policy objectives nor easy to predict when or whether such activity will diminish. Pressure from the US may have some effect on Chinese cyber espionage, and Beijing's interest in improving the legality and hygiene of the Chinese internet could constrain the behaviour of non-state actors, while causing state actors to be more discriminating in their selection of targets. But it is safe to assume that China will continue to resort to cyber espionage to secure national advantage – just as most other states do – and will seek to silence foreign-based dissidents.

By the same token, China will attempt to exploit the full potential of the cyber domain in enabling and enhancing military capabilities that it benchmarks against those of the US. The Chinese leadership still sees cyberspace as something of an Achilles heel for an American military that is heavily dependent on networked communications and systems – even while, ironically, the People's Liberation Army acquires many of these vulnerabilities through its own Revolution in Military Affairs with Chinese Characteristics. The PLA has an ambitious cyber agenda but, like most militaries, it is struggling to integrate cyber capabilities into its doctrines and practices. And, although it regards such capabilities as having the potential to create military outcomes with reduced risks and casualty rates, the PLA is likely to be cautious about deploying them unless it has unwavering confidence in their effectiveness. However, the history of the Chinese way of war suggests that, if China does engage in hostilities, it will deploy the full spectrum of capabilities from the outset – meaning that cyber attacks would be a key component of any major assault. The PLA has invested heavily in fibre-optic networks within China, and may have calculated that, in the event of a conflict with a major competitor such as the US military, it could seek to inflict maximum damage on American ICT networks before retreating behind a virtual barricade and relying on an intranet largely immune from foreign interference.

The evolution of China's cyber power epitomises the challenges inherent in the country's emergence as a major global power. Having swiftly, if belatedly, adopted what was once a quintessentially Western technology, China is now increasingly trying to impose its stamp on that technology and the way that it is used. And this will have global implications if, as seems probable, Chinese cyber influence continues to grow. The challenge for Western policymakers is firstly to understand what China is trying to do and why, and then to think through the relevant implications. The US and its allies also need to consider what might constitute realistic red lines for a technology that is developing rapidly and in ways that are difficult to predict. This process requires a shift in mindset towards appreciating that the West's long-standing technological edge is fast eroding and can no longer be taken for granted. Of course, there is no guarantee that China will achieve its national ambitions within the cyber domain: in the long run, technological development could outstrip the imperatives of political control. However, it would be unwise to count on such an outcome. In the case of China's cyber power and ambitions, doing so would be a major strategic error.

It is hard to imagine the contours of a global cyber domain shaped in China's image. But, to the extent that country's positions become global norms, there will be an acceleration of an already apparent trend towards the fragmentation of the internet, whereby the availability of online information varies markedly from state to state. In China's case, this could well be accompanied by greater extraterritorial application of its own laws in an attempt to silence critics of the leadership. As China's economic influence increases, states may be increasingly reluctant to offend the Chinese leadership and hence responsive to Chinese pressure to suppress unwelcome narratives. At the same time, the Chinese view of the world is likely to become more prevalent as China seeks to expand its overseas propaganda efforts and projection of 'soft power'. Beijing will also continue its efforts to shape global internet architecture and engineering standards, in the hope of acquiring some of the influence and leverage enjoyed by the US. At worst, this trend could lead to the emergence of a world characterised by competing cyber camps between whom there is limited connectivity, and who develop offensive cyber capabilities behind virtual walls. But it is likely that China would wish to avoid such an extreme scenario, if at all possible, given its enduring emphasis on economic development – and its historical awareness of the dangers of isolationism. For now, China appears to believe that it can have its cake and eat it: gaining the economic benefits that come with global connectivity while excluding information seen as detrimental to political and social stability. The country has in effect embarked on a global experiment in which liberal democracies serve as the control group. It will be some time before any safe conclusions can be reached about this experiment.

Notes

1 话说天下大势合久必分，分久必合.

2 'China "Social Credit": Beijing Sets Up Huge System', BBC, 26 October 2015.

3 'State IT Firm, Microsoft to Co-Produce OS', Xinhua, 17 December 2015.

INDEX

Adelphi books are published eight times a year by Routledge Journals, an imprint of Taylor & Francis, 4 Park Square, Milton Park, Abingdon, Oxfordshire OX14 4RN, UK.

A subscription to the institution print edition, ISSN 1944-5571, includes free access for any number of concurrent users across a local area network to the online edition, ISSN 1944-558X. Taylor & Francis has a flexible approach to subscriptions enabling us to match individual libraries' requirements. This journal is available via a traditional institutional subscription (either print with free online access, or online-only at a discount) or as part of our libraries, subject collections or archives. For more information on our sales packages please visit www.tandfonline.com/librarians_pricinginfo_journals.

2016 Annual Adelphi Subscription Rates			
Institution	£651	$1,144 USD	€965
Individual	£230	$393 USD	€314
Online only	£570	$1,001 USD	€844

Dollar rates apply to subscribers outside Europe. Euro rates apply to all subscribers in Europe except the UK and the Republic of Ireland where the pound sterling price applies. All subscriptions are payable in advance and all rates include postage. Journals are sent by air to the USA, Canada, Mexico, India, Japan and Australasia. Subscriptions are entered on an annual basis, i.e. January to December. Payment may be made by sterling cheque, dollar cheque, international money order, National Giro, or credit card (Amex, Visa, Mastercard).

For a complete and up-to-date guide to Taylor & Francis journals and books publishing programmes, and details of advertising in our journals, visit our website: http://www.tandfonline.com.

Ordering information:
USA/Canada: Taylor & Francis Inc., Journals Department, 530 Walnut Street, Suite 850, Philadelphia, PA 19106, USA. **UK/Europe/Rest of World:** Routledge Journals, T&F Customer Services, T&F Informa UK Ltd., Sheepen Place, Colchester, Essex, CO3 3LP, UK.

Advertising enquiries to:
USA/Canada: The Advertising Manager, Taylor & Francis Inc., 530 Walnut Street, Suite 850, Philadelphia, PA 19106, USA. Tel: +1 (800) 354 1420. Fax: +1 (215) 207 0050. **UK/Europe/Rest of World:** The Advertising Manager, Routledge Journals, Taylor & Francis, 4 Park Square, Milton Park, Abingdon, Oxfordshire OX14 4RN, UK. Tel: +44 (0) 20 7017 6000. Fax: +44 (0) 20 7017 6336.

The print edition of this journal is printed on ANSI conforming acid-free paper by Bell & Bain, Glasgow, UK.